*Everything You Need to
Know to Play Wall Street's
Hottest Game!*

How to
Get Started in
Electronic
Day Trading

David S. Nassar

McGraw-Hill

New York   San Francisco   Washington, D.C.   Auckland   Bogotá
Caracas   Lisbon   London   Madrid   Mexico City   Milan
Montreal   New Delhi   San Juan   Singapore
Sydney   Tokyo   Toronto

Library of Congress Catalog-in-Publication Data

Nassar, David S.
How to get started in electronic day trading :
    everything you need to know to play Wall Street's hottest
    game / David S. Nassar.
New York : McGraw-Hill, 1999.
p. cm.
HG4515.95
0071345663
Electronic trading of securities.
Stocks — Data processing.
98040807

McGraw-Hill

A Division of The McGraw·Hill Companies

0 DOC/DOC 9 0 3 2 1 0 9

ISBN 0-07-134566-3

Printed and bound by R.R. Donnelley & Sons Company.

McGraw-Hill books are available at special quantity discounts to use as premiums and sales promotions, or for use in corporate training programs. For
more information, please write to the Director of Special Sales, McGraw-Hill,
11 West 19th Street, New York, NY 10011. Or contact your local bookstore.

 This book is printed on recycled, acid-free paper containing a minimum of 50% recycled de-inked fiber.

CONTENTS

To my sons, Zachary and Weston, the real future of trading!

INTRODUCTION

A tsunami—spawned by technological breakthroughs, new regulations, more savvy individual traders, and even the Crash of '87—is striking the securities industry. A 23-foot wave of virtual water moving at 186,300 miles per second is flooding the innermost sanctums of Wall Street even as you read this book. Until very recently, direct electronic access to the exchanges was taboo, and the gates of Wall Street were closed to the public. For over 200 years of the stock market's history, industry professionals have been a very esoteric club. Now the markets open are for the execution of orders sent directly to them by traders sitting in front of their personal computers anywhere in the world. You can surf the crest of this virtual wave—any time you want from any Internet access point on the planet!

It is open season on Wall Street. Point to a stock on your computer screen, click your mouse, and seconds later you have bought or sold that stock. It is that fast, easy, and efficient. If you have a passion for the market and are not already utilizing the technology and strategies available to access it directly, this book will show you how.

For the first time ever, you can trade directly with the specialists of the New York Stock Exchange and NASDAQ market makers. The most important word is *directly*. No telephone calls to your broker. No waiting for a trader's wire. No lost time as your broker relays your orders to the firm's order desk. No delay as the order desk moves your orders to the trading floor or a stock wholesaler. No "paid-for order flow." No delay getting your fills, or executions. You shortcut the entire process by firing your orders *directly*:

Point . . . Click . . . Buy!

Point . . . Click . . . Sell!

This isn't the on-line trading many of the large retail and discount brokers have been making noise about lately. All they provide is a glorified e-mail service. You send their trade rooms something similar to an e-mail message, telling them how many shares you want to buy or sell. They in turn handle your orders as if you telephoned them in, just as it has been done for decades.

Worse yet, many sell your order to a broker's broker to fill, a practice known as "paid-for order flow." A broker's broker is a security wholesaler who buys your orders from your broker, along with hundreds of thousands of other orders and matches them up. Your buy completes someone else's sell. There is nothing illegal about this practice, except that you do not always get the best price possible. The broker's brokers, or security wholesalers, earn the spread between your order and the one it is matched with. The spread could be an eighth of a point or more and that is not acceptable in today's efficient stock market, especially for short-term strategies. Electronic direct access trading (E-DAT) allows you to buy and sell at the best prices the market has to offer.

When you trade with an on-line system, you may think that you are getting a good deal because your commission is less than $20. But if you pay an unnecessary spread, an eighth of a point costs you an additional $125 on a thousand-share trade. Therefore, you actually paid $145, with the commission and spread, or an extra $32.50 on a hundred lot. Your brokerage firm receives perhaps a penny and a half a share for selling your orders. They charged you $20 and are paid $15 from the broker's broker (1000 shares × $0.015). To avoid being known as a firm that takes payment for orders, some discounters have bought their wholesaler, but the order's path is the same. And so is the result for the trader—higher buys and lower sells. Routing your orders directly through an E-DAT system via various execution mediums can save you money on those spreads!

PROFIT ON A "TEENIE" . . . REALLY?

E-DAT allows you to bypass all the middlepeople and route your orders to the exchange using several different order-entry systems.

This book will teach you how to use these systems. You will be able to profit on moves as small as one-sixteenth, referred to as a *teenie* or a steenth in the industry. A teenie is all of six and one-quarter cents per share. This book will teach you how deep discount commissions, new rules, and technology will make E-DAT the future of trading! Learn to:

- Route your orders **directly** to the specialists on the New York Stock Exchange
- Pick off buys and sells **directly** from the market makers
- Get fills in as little as one second
- Unlock markets Wall Street has made inaccessible to you until recently
- Tap into information previously not available to anyone outside the securities industry
- Make money on teenies on 1000-share lots, and
- Execute lightning-fast, low-cost trades with professional trading systems

There has not been an opportunity like this for the average person to trade stocks since the last century. Those were the days of Jesse Livermore, often renowned as the greatest stock speculator ever. There were trading offices on every corner and even in the lobbies of most hotels. You could walk into establishments referred to as "bucket shops," place orders on margin, and get fills immediately, using the price right off the telegraph's ticker tape. Only recently have individual traders begun to see fast fills and low commissions like those. The irony of market accessibility of the past and technology of today can be credited to the NASDAQ.

NASDAQ was the first "screen-based market." Through technology and computers, it paved the way for other electronic systems, such as the Electronic Communication Networks (ECNs), SOES, SelectNet, and the order-routing system of the NYSE, SuperDot. All of this will be explained in detail in this book. Without these systems, individual traders would not be able to trade **directly** via the Internet or any other means. Fortress Wall Street would still command the trading floors. NASDAQ is the greatest breakthrough in the last two centuries for individual traders. As revolutionary as NASDAQ is, new systems are still coming on-line. One such screen-based system is OptiMark, which has the potential to challenge the dominance of even the New York Stock Exchange. More on this later.

Many times problems become opportunity, and the "crash of '87" was the next big break for Electronic Direct Access Trading. The Dow Jones Industrial Average was hammered down more than 500 points on October 19, 1987. Customers could not get through to their brokers. Brokerage phones rang off their hooks. The day seemed as if it would never end—panic and fear ruled the day. The very next day, opportunists swept in from Wall Street to take fast profits. They cashed in, big time!

The combination of these events and others helped change the landscape of the NASDAQ, through changes made by the Justice Department and the SEC. Systems already in place, giving individual traders direct access to the markets, became mandatory. New rules were instituted to bring the public and the professionals into equilibrium. Now you have the same opportunity as the professional trading community. All these reforms took place just as the securities industry and individual traders embraced the technological innovations that had been around for years. It all came together. NASDAQ, the Internet, 56K modems, satellites, Electronic Communications Networks, E-DAT schools—all the pieces of the puzzle fell in place. In this book you will learn how to marry these technological marvels with proven trading strategies that will change the way people trade and invest forever! Welcome to the "Bleeding Edge!"

THE ELECTRONIC DAY TRADER IS BORN!

First, let me define what day trading really is. Day trading is not necessarily trading every day as much as it is being in "tune" with the market every day. One of many approaches to take advantage of these new rules and technology is known as *electronic scalping*.

Traditional scalpers are traders who buy and sell rapidly for their own account, taking small profits and limiting losses, holding positions for very short periods of time. Scalpers generally trade "heavy," meaning a high number of shares for small, incremental profits per trade. Typically, scalpers stand ready to buy at a fraction below the last transaction price and sell at a fraction above the next, harnessing small tidy little profits throughout a trading day. In short, they hit base hits, not home runs.

Until now, it has been almost impossible for anyone to compete and trade with the NASDAQ market makers as a scalper because of market barriers, such as rules, technology, and high commissions. That has all changed with the advent of electronic direct access trading. Done properly by traders with the right equipment and training, it is a way of taking a considerable amount of profit from the market. For example, you buy 1000 shares of a stock and hold it for a minute or two. If it can be sold for a 1/4-point above what you paid, or even less, you take fast profit (less commissions).

Do that successfully every trading day and you begin to wonder why you waited until now to start. E-DAT scalpers can be full- or part-timers. Some do it professionally and others just to supplement their current income. The new rules, new technology, and deep discount commissions available today make E-DAT scalping a very real opportunity for the serious trader or investor.

You do not have to be an E-DAT scalper to enjoy the opportunities offered by this new revolution in trading. There is a whole spectrum of different types of electronic traders, such as day traders, who hold positions for a few minutes to a few hours; swing traders who hold positions one to five days, and many hybrids of these methods. In fact, there seem to be as many styles of trading as there are personalities. Traditional "buy 'n' hold" investors also use this type of trading, because they understand how it gets them the very best price whenever they buy or sell. They can trade through E-DAT brokers, account executives trained in electronic direct access trading. These brokers trade directly on E-DAT systems to shave spreads for customers. But don't try to find these brokers at traditional retail brokerage houses. They know how to shave an eighth or a quarter of a point off for their customers. They offer deep discount commissions and help you save on the spread. By the time you finish this book, you will know how to do this yourself or at least know enough to look for a brokerage firm with proficient E-DAT brokers.

Before you quit your day job, read this book carefully. You'll learn all you need to know to decide if you are mentally and psychologically suited for electronic trading. Not everyone is, although just about anyone who invests in the stock market can benefit by using E-DAT. Jessie Livermore probably stated it best back in 1923: "The game of speculation is the most uniformly fascinating game in the world. But it is not a game for the stupid, the mentally lazy, the man [or woman] of inferior emotional balance, nor for the get-rich-quick adventurer. They will die poor."

STRUCTURE OF THIS BOOK

The text is divided into three main parts. Chapters 1 through 5 cover all the key areas you must become familiar with to successfully trade electronically. For example, you will learn the secrets of the exchanges, all about the electronic order execution systems and how to use them, the special rules governing electronic trading, which indexes can be used as leading price indicators, and how to get an edge with technical analysis. Most importantly, you will come to understand just how NASDAQ market makers think, so you can anticipate how they trade. Once you can do that, you can run with these market movers and enjoy the profits the market has to offer rather than being stampeded by them.

The next section, Chapters 6 through 10, puts you in the middle of the fray. You will define your trading style and time horizon of trading. Trading styles are as different as people. This section will help you define what kind of trader you will become. Your time horizon can be anywhere from a few minutes to a few days. I will then teach you several of the most reliable trading strategies known to E-DAT traders. There are trading opportunities that are predictable days and sometimes weeks in advance and others that just come at you without warning. With hard work you will begin to see these trends.

The book concludes with an overview of the mechanics of setting up an electronic stock trading account and a grand finale of the best, most useful, advice I have learned about E-DAT trading over the years I have been trading and teaching others. If you can learn from others' mistakes, this section can save you thousands of dollars, by showing you how not to lose your money: the first lesson to successful trading no matter how or where you trade.

I also recommend that you peruse the Afterword and the Appendixes. The Afterword provides my insights into the ever-changing electronic trading world. The future is very bright. A new trading platform, called OptiMark, may well become the ultimate electronic specialist or market maker—providing price improvement for average traders. This system has the potential to offer you a far better trading field than the average trader has ever had access to. It is difficult to say just how lucky we all are to be trading at this particular time in history. Last of all are the Appendixes, which are packed with helpful reference material.

That's the book in a nutshell. Reading it is like reaching for your mouse and opening a window on the World Wide Web. One click leads to another and before you know it you will be prepared to take advantage of the incredible opportunities you have as an Electronic Direct Access Trader.

WELCOME

Electronic Direct Access Trading (E-DAT), while new to the landscape of the market, is really nothing more than a technological improvement on trading styles and disciplines enjoyed by professional traders for years. The E-DAT today will implement psychology, human nature, and common sense to trade not too much unlike the professional trader from years ago.

On the other hand, the technology available today is so innovative that most still do not understand the differences between on-line trading and the true Electronic Direct Access Trading Industry. Never before has the public had the keys to the gate of the most fascinating financial institution in the world, the U.S. STOCK MARKET!

Thanks to "bleeding edge" computer technology, you now have those keys to unlock the gate to the professional trading market. From your home computer you can interface directly to the NASDAQ, NYSE, and other exchanges, to create a virtual market in cyberspace. "Screen Based Markets" such as the NASDAQ have made way for mediums to view the market tick for tick, trade for trade, in real time. Real-time executions allow you to act on this direct information with the press of a mouse or keyboard. This level of technology has attracted an unprecedented number of traders and investors to the market, and research has proven that this industry is still an infant. Yet unfortunately, many will become victims of the markets because the education, knowledge, and skills to act with confidence are often missing.

I hope that you see this book as a step to change that. We are all students of this industry regardless of our skill or experience. In fact, there are two kinds of traders: the ones who admit they lose trades, and then the ones who are liars. All traders lose trades; it's part of the profession, just like a good quarterback throwing interceptions. The champions just don't let the turnovers defeat them or their attitudes; and herein lies the secret to trading. Developing a positive attitude and overcoming fear is the real art, and you will learn how!

The discipline you develop along with proven trading strategies in this book using "Real Time" data is the winning combination necessary to play in Wall Street's hottest game. This powerful system will allow you to access the exchanges directly without anyone ever touching your order. When *you* point and *you* click, *you* own! That fast. That quick. That powerful.

Electronic trading could be compared to law or medicine in that many disciplines and strategies are available, but specializing in just a few is all it takes; a new doctor or attorney will specialize. The market is certainly dynamic, but with your passion and willingness to learn everyday, you too can have the power and technology to interact with the most vibrant profit generator on the planet!

David S. Nassar

ACKNOWLEDGMENTS

I would like to thank Stephen Isaacs of McGraw-Hill Professional Publishing for giving me the opportunity to write this book. I also want to thank Kevin Ward for his market insights and Jason Turnipseed for his exceptional effort every day! Thank you, Tom McCafferty, for all your hard work on this book.

Thanks to Dr. Jack Bauersachs for his thoughts from the academic perspective and to Mark Marone and Robin Peterson for their support and friendship.

Thank you, Myron Klingensmith, for teaching our E-DAT Trading Courses like the true professional you are. My thanks to Stan Yan, a fellow trader and artist, who did an outstanding job creating the illustrations.

To Gabbiel E. Nassar, Sr., and Glenna A. Nassar, two people I am proud to call my parents.

And finally, the most special thanks to my family, my wife, Tracy, and my sons, Zachary and Weston, for their patience and support during the busy time of writing this book.

DISCLAIMER

This book is intended for educational purposes only. It is expressly understood that this book is not in any way intended to give investment advice or recommendations to trade stock or any other investment. The author and publisher assume no responsibilities for the investment results obtained by the reader from relying on the information contained in this book. Investing is inherently risky and results obtained by some investors may not be obtained or obtainable by other investors in similar or dissimilar conditions. The reader assumes the entire risk of investing, trading, or buying and selling securities. The author or publisher shall have no liability for any loss or expense whatsoever relating to investment decisions made by the reader.

1

THE MAJOR MARKETS AND THEIR ELECTRONIC TRADING SYSTEMS

lectronic direct access trading (E-DAT) means using your computer to trade *directly* with those people or entities that can buy stock from you or sell stock to you. These are the specialists on the listed exchanges, NASDAQ market makers, and electronic communications networks (ECNs) that match electronic traders to buy and sell directly with each other. E-DAT is *not* just on-line trading.

The key word is *direct*. No one ever touches your order until it reaches a place where it can be filled. No broker. No trading-desk. There is nothing between your orders and your fills. That is a hard concept for many traditional stock traders to comprehend. It is the only way, in my opinion, an average person can successfully day trade for short periods of time and for small, incremental profits. E-DAT also enables traders to take advantage of rumors and news-driven events that cause stocks to move quickly and abruptly while producing executions in as little as one second.

Up until recently, market professionals had the advantage. Average investor-traders had no way of accessing the key factors that would show them the intraday momentum of individual stocks in real time. More importantly, traders could not execute orders fast enough or cheaply enough to make profits from small price changes. Nor could they close their positions within seconds to protect themselves if the stocks headed in the wrong direction.

Now things are very different. As it usually does, change came as the result of some extremely traumatic events. Where were you on October 19, 1987? To serious traders, it is like asking baby boomers where they were the day President John Kennedy was shot. The nineteenth was the day the phones rang and rang and rang. The Dow-Jones average dropped over 500 points and hardly 1 stockbroker in 10 was in their offices. Or, at least that is how it felt as investors tried to call in exit orders. Today, if you do not dump unwanted shares instantaneously by using the technology available, you have no one to blame but yourself.

The less than stellar performance of the brokerage community eventually compelled the Securities and Exchange Commission (SEC) to make some changes. The most recognized example was the mandatory participation of the market makers in the Small Order Execution System (SOES), which was already in place. This execution system allows customers to send orders directly to the markets, even if their brokers do not answer their phones. This first change was the catalyst for many more to come. Additionally, some very important order-handling rules, for example, the Limit Order Protection Rule, were initiated in 1996. This book explains these changes in detail and teaches you how to take advantage of them, so you can trade directly at light speed and compete with the Wall Street professionals at their own game.

The wheels of change do not turn quickly or easily. It took considerable time and many bureaucratic changes to bring electronic direct access to the public. But all that hassle is in the rear view mirror and this book is about the future, which has never been brighter for the individual stock trader or investor. You, as an electronic trader, will be at the bleeding edge of technology as we prepare to enter the twenty-first century.

To understand how to use these new tools, you need some background on the markets, their information systems, and how orders can be executed directly to the markets. You have access to four primary electronic order-entry and routing systems: the NYSE's SuperDot, the NASDAQ's SOES and SelectNet, and the six independent Electronic Communications Networks (ECNs). I like to think of these as your weapon systems for shooting down profits.

The market in which securities are bought and sold is known as the *secondary market*, as opposed to the *primary market* for new issues, or initial public offerings (IPOs). Once a stock passes through the IPO process, it is sold either on a listed securities exchange or on the over-the-counter (OTC) market. The primary difference between the exchanges and OTC markets is in the way trading is conducted. The exchanges are centralized, and a specialist maintains an auction market between buyers and sellers. The OTC market is decentralized and market makers compete among themselves as well as the public. It is important to understand the difference between how these two markets conduct transactions.

SCOPE OF NEW YORK STOCK EXCHANGE

The largest and most well-known listed stock exchange is the New York Stock Exchange (NYSE). Since it functions in principally the same manner as the other regional exchanges, and is significantly more liquid, only this exchange will be discussed. The NYSE handles over three-fourths of all stock transactions occurring on all the listed exchanges. Companies listed on the NYSE have larger capitalization and tend to be more mature than those listed on the over-the-counter markets. These corporations also tend to be more interested in generating dividends for shareholders, while the NASDAQ companies are more growth-oriented.

The NYSE utilizes a specialist system within its auction market. The primary function of the stock specialist system is to maintain a fair and orderly market for a particular stock. There is one specialist for each stock on each exchange—one person who directs order flow.

To achieve their primary function, specialists act as both brokers and dealers. As *brokers,* they execute orders left them by other members or orders routed to them electronically by customers of numerous member firms. As *dealers*, they execute orders for their own accounts, taking small profits while maintaining liquidity. The specialist does not have to be a party in every transaction occurring in their stock, but transactions on the floor of the exchange do take place in front of them as well as on their computer terminals, and therefore give the specialist a broad perspective of the entire order flow of the stock at any given moment. This advantage will determine if the market in the stock is a net buyer's or a net seller's market, and therefore will show the specialist where the stock is heading. This one person system gives the specialist an advantage and a responsibility to provide a liquid market.

To find liquidity for buyers and sellers, specialists can quote the stock in which they specialize, in order to bring out sellers when demand is high or buyers when demand is low. This ability to manage the order flow is the most important aspect of the specialist's job. The specialist is like an auctioneer, raising and lowering prices to elicit a response from the floor brokers and traders. By lowering prices, buyers may step in and become the liquidity for sellers, or the effect may also increase panic in the market and actually bring out more sellers, and cause even more imbalance of buyers to sellers. The point is, the specialist has the power to rally, retard, or halt a stock. Because this power exists for the specialist, he or she is also responsible for keeping a high degree of fairness and order in the stock. Often you will see a delayed opening or a halt in trading of a listed stock, which is a valuable tool of the specialist to employ when order is compromised, such as when unexpected rumors or news rocks a stock he or she specializes in.

The specialist function is not present in NASDAQ, which utilizes a multiple market maker system. Because it is an electronic screen-based market, not located in a single physical location, as are the NYSE and other regional exchanges, it is fractured and much less controllable. See Figures 1.1 and 1.2. Its market makers compete fiercely in bloody negotiations—all attempting to make a profit on the same stocks at the same time. This is why the NASDAQ is known as a *negotiated market*. Traditionally, market makers contacted each

FIGURE 1-1 *For the first time since the stock exchanges began trading over 200 years ago, the average investor/trader can place orders directly with the specialists of the listed exchanges and the market makers of the over-the-counter, screen-based markets. Your orders can be sent directly to an entity that can actually sell stock directly to you or buy it from you.*

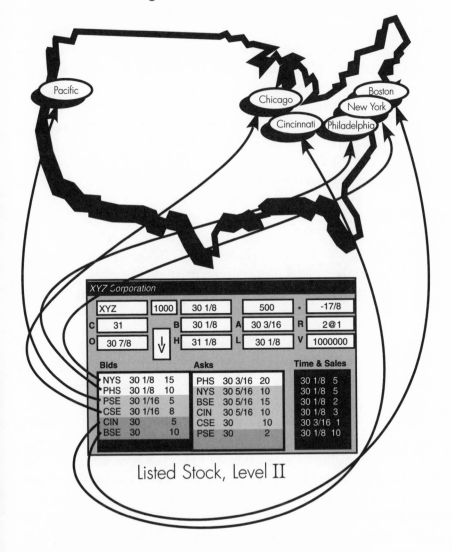

Listed Exchanges Are Centralized Locations

Listed Stock, Level II

other to buy and sell stock for customers and their own account. Because of this multiple market maker system, they negotiate and compete with each other. Listed securities is not a multiple system and is controlled by one auctioneer called the "specialist."

Market makers on the NASDAQ generally make markets in several stocks and compete with other market makers for order flow in those stocks to fill their customers' orders or trade for their own behalf. On the NYSE, stock specialists are responsible for maintaining an orderly market in a single stock. This means these specialists must buy during descending markets, when there are more sellers than buyers. When the buyers outnumber the sellers, the specialists must sell into ascending markets. Specialists can do this and stay solvent because they can sell out of their inventory. The exchange also provides special concessions to make their function a profitable one, such as the ability to see all the order flow of buyers and sellers. The specialists must repay this favorable treatment by maintaining high standards of ethical conduct, which in my opinion they do very well.

Another big difference is the way these two entities handle the actual buying and selling of shares. The NYSE is an auction market as I noted earlier. Floor brokers present all orders to the specialists by open outcry. The specialist is the auctioneer, handling the bids and asks. Today's volume, combined with the specialization that has taken place over its 200+ years, has modified this approach somewhat, but that is how it was designed to work and basically still does.

NASDAQ, on the other hand, was designed for subscribers to make bids and offers. It is a negotiated market. The subscribers bargain with one another via their computer screens to arrive at price equilibrium or levels where buyers match with sellers and vice versa. Because there is no open outcry and a multiple market maker system, market makers will attempt to hide their intentions and buy stock when others are selling due to perceived weakness, and sell while others are buying due to perceived strength. Those who do it best make handsome profits. On the NYSE, it is not as easy for the public to see where the money is flowing, and therefore it is not considered a "transparent" market as is the NASDAQ. Although market makers will attempt to hide their intentions, because there are so many in most NASDAQ stocks, they do become "transparent" through a system I will soon introduce called "Level II."

Think of it this way: It's like telling only your best friend a secret; if your friend tells no one your secret is secure. If he/she tells a few others, the grapevine effect is born and something leaks. That's what the specialist is like, your best friend who tells no one, and therefore stock prices tend to move with less manipulation because there is less transparency and therefore less chance for the stock to trade with volatility. The one specialist system creates more security in determining money flow, i.e., more buying than selling, vise versa. The NASDAQ is the grapevine effect, *multiple* market makers all trying to be incognito, but actually as a whole can be studied to show the astute observer where the money is flowing. Too many know the secret, and therefore the leak will occur. Multiple market makers will show you the secret of where a stock is heading many times by watching how they bid to buy, or offer to sell, stock.

All these differences are critical to electronic traders. The NYSE specialists function as price monitors. This has a calming effect on the market and usually reduces price volatility, allowing short-term traders to hold their positions longer. The same E-DAT traders on NASDAQ would be looking for a much faster turnaround. A study on very short-term trading conducted by Jeffrey H. Harris of the University of Notre Dame and Paul H. Schultz of Ohio State University in July 1997 suggested that a SOES trader's success rate trading the NASDAQ drops substantially after holding a position longer than two minutes. Short-term trading, of course, is not, and should not be, the only game played on the NASDAQ's trading screens, but this study shows how quickly inefficiency is corrected on the NASDAQ.

A news-driven event that truly gets the public's attention is a good example of the inefficiency and volatility that can occur on NASDAQ. Assume some announcement was made about a breakthrough regarding a new generation of computer chips over the weekend. On Monday, you would find the NASDAQ market makers bidding the company's stock higher among themselves because they would suspect that there would be plenty of market orders for the open on Monday. The market makers do not have the luxury of delaying the opening of a stock, as the specialists do on a listed stock. There are just too many market makers making a market in any one stock. This is fundamentally different than the case of listed stocks where only one specialist per exchange controls a stock. As a result of this fundamental difference, the market makers will protect themselves by going extra high on the bid, because they don't want to be caught selling the stock too low when news rocks a stock, as in this example. Therefore, often the price will be artificially high. No market maker will want to be low bid on the stock, because they expect the poor unsuspecting public will rush in to buy it.

Often in these situations, the market makers will not have enough stock to sell so they sell the stock short (to be explained later) to fill the demand. When the market makers have their own money at risk (and they hate risk), they will protect themselves by bidding the stock artificially high. As they sell the overpriced stock to the public, they know they can buy it back much cheaper after price equilibrium is established. Once market makers run out of buyers, the stock "tanks." The public, who rush in, lose out because the average purchaser does not understand how the market makers work on the NASDAQ. Understanding the nuances of the listed exchanges and the NASDAQ market will allow you to avoid situations like this.

What would have happened on the NYSE? All the orders would have gone to the specialist of that stock. That specialist probably would have delayed the opening until the situation could be sorted out. Now there would still have been a big pop at the opening, but probably not anything like what happens on NASDAQ. The trader must be aware of how these markets can act differently to the same type of news. Neither market is perfect or right—they just do things differently. Adjusting to the personality of each market is another lesson all traders need to learn.

SUPERDOT

The NYSE's computerized routing system is called SuperDot, an acronym for Super Designated Order Turnaround. Orders can be routed directly to the appropriate specialist, or the exchange member can send it to the brokerage firm's house post for handling. Once the specialist or commission broker receives the order, it is presented in the auction market. It is estimated that as much as 50 percent of all orders traded on the NYSE go through SuperDot; program trading has a lot to do with this.

As a rule of thumb, smaller orders are handled by SuperDot. To assure they are well represented in the market, floor brokers deliver larger orders directly to the specialist. These floor brokers have good relationships with their customers and work hard for the customers. They try to direct customers to buy or sell by what they see on the floor in terms of momentum. The advantage of being on the floor is seeing what is happening through the outcry system. This system is referred to as an "outcry" because traders are physically yelling commands to the specialist. A good floor broker will use this insight to direct the trading of his or her customers. If the broker is not doing the job well, the customer stops sending orders through the firm and the floor broker.

When orders are executed through SuperDot, the same automated routing system sends the execution reports back to the firm, which then notifies the registered representatives. They notify the customers of their fills. Orders executed through SuperDot are often confirmed in less than seven seconds via an E-DAT system. This speed, coupled with low-cost executions, makes trading for small price changes exciting and profitable. Now, you can trade directly, even on the NYSE. You can send your orders via SuperDot *directly* to the designated specialist. Small orders can be quickly matched by the specialist and filled in seconds. Orders are crossed, or matched, with another buyer or seller through SuperDot once the specialist confirms an execution by simply pressing a button. That's what accounts for the unbelievable speed.

One of the characteristics I really like about SuperDot is that you can sometimes improve the prices you get. For example, if a specialist is cleaning up a large order, he or she may have been given some price discretion. Let's say IBM is trading at $120 and the specialist has an order to buy a million shares. The customer tells the specialist that he or she can go as high as $123 to get the job done. The specialist has $3 or 3-points discretion. A seller, in a similar situation, may also give the specialist discretion on the downside, allowing the specialist to go lower in price to fill the entire order.

This is an opportunity for a small buyer, for example, with a limit order to buy at 120 or better to get filled at 119⅞ because the specialist is anxious to clear the books. Or a seller with a limit order, to sell at 120 or better, gets filled at 120⅛. These are examples of what is known as *price improvement* that is possible on SuperDot.

A new system coming out for the large institutions and small traders alike, called OptiMark, will allow the small trader, trading 1000 shares or more, to share in the liquidity of large orders. Because of the anonymous nature of the system it may, in time, even supersede and improve the SuperDot system. OptiMark's potential is so powerful that I predict the liquidity of the NYSE will be directly affected, since this system will create a medium for all institutions and traders to come together and enhance liquidity, which is the true cornerstone of an efficient market. Nevertheless, SuperDot is an excellent routing system for the small trader to trade directly on the NYSE.

CIRCUIT BREAKER RULES OR TRADING CURBS

As a final note, many people ask about trading curbs. If the Dow Jones Industrial Average (DJIA) increases or decreases by 50 points within one day, the NYSE restricts program trading and index arbitrage by professional traders. This is referred to as the "curbs," and it forces institutions to shut down their computerized trading programs. Arbitrage is simultaneously purchasing one security, such as a bundle of stocks, and selling another security, say a futures index like the S&P, in order to profit from the temporary misalignment in their prices. These programs are covered in greater detail in Chapter 3.

Additionally, the rules state that if the DJIA falls 350 points within one day, all trading on the exchange halts for half an hour. If the DJIA continues to decline by 550 points, trading halts for one hour.

Summary

- The NYSE is an auction market.
- There is one specialist for each stock per exchange.
- All order flow is "presented" to the specialist. Small orders generally go through SuperDot, while larger orders are represented on the floor by floor brokers.
- Typically large cap stocks are traded.
- Listed corporations are more interested in paying dividends than plowing all profits into growth.
- NYSE issues tend to be less volatile than NASDAQ stocks.

SCOPE OF NASDAQ

The over-the-counter market is the oldest and largest continuously functioning securities market in the world. Broker-dealers, aka market makers, negotiate trades directly with one another. The OTC market entails thousands and thousands of stocks. Most of these stocks are too small and the trading is too light for these stocks to be listed on any exchange.

The most visible portion of the OTC market, and the newest, is NASDAQ, the National Association of Securities Dealers Automated Quotations system, created in February 1971. It is a screen-based stock market, or interdealer communications network linking broker-dealers through telephone and data lines. NASDAQ provides price quotations and market-making services for a wide variety of securities, but this book focuses on common stock.

For the E-DAT trader, the NASDAQ is transparent. This means that all the market markers are visible to the subscribers of a Level II system, which is described in the next section. This is not the case with the NYSE, which enjoys the benefit of more confidentiality by having only one specialist per stock per exchange. Momentum trading is much more viable on the NASDAQ due to its transparency. Traders can watch the movement of the market makers, predict their motivation, and try to trade with, or shadow, their moves.

The market makers are charged with many of the same responsibilities as the specialist on the NYSE. For example, they must make a two-sided market in the stocks for which they are registered as market makers. A two-sided market means they must be willing to buy and to sell stock at the price they quote. They quote their intentions on Level II, and whatever bid and ask price they quote, they must honor. Their third responsibility is to show the number of shares they are willing to buy (bid) and sell (ask or offer) at the price they post on the Level II screen.

For example, a market maker might bid 35 for 1000 shares. This simply means this market maker is willing to buy at least 1000 shares at $35. The other side of this two-way market is the ask. This is the price at which the market maker is willing to sell stock. The natural spread between these two prices is the riskless spread market makers have been enjoying for years. In this example, the market maker would likely quote the ask or offer at 35⅛ for 1000 shares, meaning sell 1000 shares for $35.125.

Seeing a Level II screen and all the market makers on both sides of the market, including prices and volume, makes the market transparent. Having access to electronic information on all the market makers is as every bit as important as being able to execute trades electronically. Think of market makers as any other dealers. If you want to buy a BMW you go to a dealer to get it. If you wish to buy 1000 shares of Dell stock, you must also do so through a dealer. Seeing what they are doing is power!

Another tool that is equally important to have is the "Time and Sale screen," which provides additional insight into NASDAQ. For the astute trader, it can equate to a much higher profit potential. This screen displays the time each transaction (a buy or a sell) takes place and the size of the transaction. Chapter 5 teaches you how to use these screens in tandem to see where money is flowing in a given stock; are the market makers net buyers or net sellers?

When you learn to read the Level II and the Time and Sale screen in concert, you begin to feel the pulse of a stock. Nevertheless, this information is still only the tip of the iceberg. The true volume of stock to be bought or sold is not known due to the multiple market maker system, and the market makers have no intention of showing it to you. Therefore, it is your ability to read the Level II and the Time and Sale screen that will define your ability to read directional bias and successful momentum trade.

A fundamental difference between the NYSE and the NASDAQ is the order flow. In the NASDAQ it is split among many market makers; in the NYSE a specialist in a given stock knows the entire order flow. Momentum trading opportunities are created by a "grapevine" effect. When too many players are involved, secrets are hard to keep; therefore, the iceberg can often be seen by careful study of the market makers. For example, they may show a bid to buy 1000 shares, but they may need 10,000 or 100,000 to fill the customer order from a mutual fund or pension fund. This is the part of the iceberg that is underwater. Your task is to study the action and reaction of the market makers to determine what is really behind what appears to be happening. If the market maker in this example spends more time at the bid, you can begin to suspect they are buyers in order to fill a large order for a customer.

NASDAQ SERVICES

The NASDAQ National Market System (NMS) is the most popular service offered to its member firm subscribers. The NASDAQ system includes current price quotations from more than 500 market makers on more than 5000 actively traded securities.

The NASDAQ system provides three levels of stock quotation services. Level I was designed for registered representatives or stockbrokers. Level II, until recently, was only available to professional trading desks in brokerage firms. It is now available to you as well. Level III is interactive and includes special features for market makers that allows them to update and revise their quotes on the Level II.

- NASDAQ Level I displays the inside market only. The inside market is the highest bid and the lowest ask. Because of normal market price fluctuations, a Level I quote, as it appears on the screen, may or may not be accurate. A registered rep cannot guarantee a Level I price to a customer. Most Internet and subscription-based quote services provide this information on a real time or delayed basis. Generally, if price quotations are delayed, the subscriber does not have to pay the exchange a fee. But if the quotes are "live," a fee is required, which adds substantially to the monthly cost.

• NASDAQ Level II traditionally was available to NASD-approved subscribers only. Only recently has the public been allowed to access it. Level II provides current quotes and the size of the quotes (number of shares being quoted at that price) available from each market maker in a particular security. Because better information means better trading, I will show you how to take maximum advantage of the additional information Level II provides. This is one of the most powerful tools you will use to trade!

FIGURE 1-2   *As an individual investor/trader, you can become a direct link in the network of security broker-dealers that make up NASDAQ. This means you can trade directly with them at the speed of light.*

NASDAQ InterDealer Networks

Broker-Dealers all connected through high-speed data lines facilitated by NASDAQ

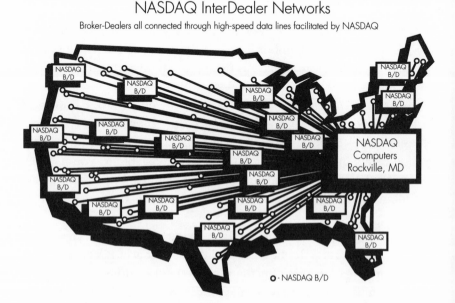

- NASDAQ Level III provides subscribers with all the services of Levels I and II and allows registered market makers to update their quotes on any security in which they make a market.

Now with ECNs and the new Limit Order Protection Rule, you too can trade like a market maker and interact with market makers in real time. This is the ultimate power. The ability to get your order on the Level II screen is a tremendous advantage E-DAT traders have over any other on-line individual traders. If you trade through a traditional broker, your ability to represent your order on a Level II is very rare at best. With electronic direct access, you can see in real time where those orders are and represent your higher bid or lower offer on Level II, also in real time. By the time your finger leaves the mouse or keyboard, your order is shown to the entire world on Level II. Representing your bid to buy or offer to sell right next to Goldman Sachs always seems to amaze new E-DATs.

These concepts are critical to understand for E-DAT traders because the Level II screen is the tool used most by short-term traders. Think in terms of wholesale and retail. If a market maker wants to buy stocks, it does it at wholesale prices (the bids). This price represents the highest price in the market that any market maker is willing to buy. It is always lower than current ask prices, which are the prices at which the market is willing to sell (retail) at the same time. That is the power of the Limit Order Protection Rule, which states that if you better the inside market you have limit order protection and a market maker cannot trade ahead of your order. This means that if you increase the high bid or decrease the low offer and your bid or offer is not filled, you become the inside bid or offer. This puts you first in line to get filled. This is possible through the use of ECNs.

THE INSIDE MARKET

The inside market is a very key issue you need to understand thoroughly before you trade directly. It is unique to NASDAQ because it utilizes a multiple market maker system, rather than a stock specialist system, such as the system on the listed exchanges. Simply put, the inside market is the best bid (highest) price at which stock can be sold in the interdealer market and the best ask (lowest) price at which the same stock can be bought. If you were a seller, wouldn't you want the highest price or high bid? And as a buyer, you would be after the cheapest price or lowest ask price. One market maker may have the best bid and another the best ask.

If you, as a trader, want to buy stocks, you want to pay as little as possible. Therefore, you would pay the "inside offer," which is the lowest price in the market that a market maker will sell at—but it is still retail. If you want to sell stocks, you want as much as possible for the stocks. The inside market is the highest price a market maker will buy at (wholesale). Anything that is not the highest bid or lowest offer is considered "outside" the market or away. In Chapter 7, I will show you how to beat even the inside market and buy at the bid (wholesale) and sell at the ask (retail), as the market makers do. I get excited just talking about it!

Remember not all OTC securities are represented on NASDAQ, many don't meet the minimum standards and are not recommended securities for E-DAT trading. The companies traded on NASDAQ, as a group, are smaller than those on the New York Stock Exchange. This also accounts for some of the added price volatility of NASDAQ.

NATIONAL ASSOCIATION OF SECURITIES DEALERS SOES AND SELECTNET

The NASD's Small Order Execution System (SOES) is an electronic order execution system, designed to facilitate the trading of small public-market orders and executable limit orders of up to 1000 shares. It is a mandatory system requiring the market maker to buy at the bid and sell at the ask. Market makers cannot refuse to take an order at their quoted price and quantity. Turning down a quote is known as "backing away from the market," and it is no longer possible because the market makers are "hit" electronically. Market makers must execute the first order that hits their bid and/or ask. Therefore, this system allows E-DAT traders to dump unwanted shares immediately. Think of SOES as an electronic dart, able to be fired by an E-DAT at market makers at "light speed."

SOES was created in 1985, but became more important after the October 19, 1987, "crash" mentioned earlier, when small investors and traders could not get out of losing positions because brokers would not answer their phones. As a result, this system revolutionized the ability of the small trader to compete on equal footing with even the largest trading rooms. It has even spawned a new verb, "to be SOESed." You'll hear it used in electronic trading brokerage houses to describe what happens to market makers when a trader "hits a bid" or "lifts an offer," meaning selling your stock to a market maker at the quoted bid and buying at the quoted offer, respectively.

Here is how it works overall:

- *Market maker registration:* All NASDAQ National Market System (NMS) market makers are required to participate in SOES. In order to be a market maker in a given stock, the market maker is required to make a two-sided market. This means they must be willing to buy stock at their posted bid and sell at their posted ask. For electronic trading purposes, this is important because it forces a market maker to buy shares from a trader if the trader wants to dump unwanted shares quickly to take a fast profit or to limit a loss. This is one of the useful risk management tools I'll discuss in detail later. The market maker doesn't know you are a novice trader making his or her first trade or a professional. SOES helps to create equilibrium between the general public and the professional trading community by executing an order against the MM's quote, who is required to honor it.
- *Clearance and settlement:* Small orders may be aggregated if the total is less than the maximum 1000 share limit, but broker-dealers may not split up large customer orders for the purpose of avoiding the 1000 share limit. This helps keep the professionals honest. Also, once a trade is done on SOES on one side of the market (buy or sell), another trade cannot be done for five minutes.

- *Restrictions:* Institutions and broker-dealers may not use the system to trade for their own accounts or for other NASD members. Only public-market and executable limit orders are acceptable. Again, the equilibrium for the E-DAT trader improves.

SELECTNET

Besides SOES, NASD also provides the SelectNet System, an electronic order-routing system. This is not a mandatory system. Market makers are not forced to buy and sell stock when using this system, as they are with SOES. Instead, SelectNet is a negotiation tool that allows market makers to communicate with each other electronically.

The SelectNet System allows E-DAT traders to buy at the bid and sell at the ask, the way a market maker would. In this situation, the trader is buying and selling directly with the market-making firms. Think of this system as being designed for market makers to use as an alternative to the telephone. Here market makers can bid or offer stocks to another market maker without having to make phone calls. Instead, they send the quote over the SelectNet System.

Only market makers receive these transmissions, they are not represented on the Level II screen the way market maker quotes are. Because these orders are not represented on the Level II screen, they do not receive limit-order protection. This means, if you make the low offer or high bid (the inside market) on the SelectNet System, the order will not show on the Level II screen the way it would if you used an ECN order. Only a market maker can initiate a SelectNet order. This is not the case with ECNs, as you will see below.

THE ECNs

Electronic Communication Networks allow you, as an E-DAT trader or investor, to bid or offer stock the way market makers do. ECNs are independent systems set up by broker-dealers to match new, incoming orders with other orders already on their system. Fills can occur in seconds. That's the NASDAQ at its best. If there is no match for your order on the system, it is posted electronically on the Level II screen, which is virtually the same as having access to the Level III market makers' screen. If you want to buy stock and the current market is 35 bid × 35⅛ asked, you can bid through an ECN at 35¹⁄₁₆ and be represented on every Level II screen in the world as the highest bidder.

Below is a listing of the ECNs currently available, in order of highest to lowest market liquidity. (Liquidity and ranking are unknown for the ECNs, Attain, RediBook, and B-Trade.) Of all the orders flowing through NASDAQ, approximately 25 percent go through ECNs. Of that 25 percent, more than three-quarters are processed on InstiNet.

1. InstiNet	INCA	Reuters system for institutions
2. Island	ISLD	Datek Trading
3. Archipelago	TNTO	AKA Terra Nova
4. B-Trade	BTRD	Bloomberg
5. RediBook	REDI	Spear, Leeds & Kellogg
6. Attain	ATTN	All-Tech Investment Group

Market makers are able to use any or all the ECNs to bid and offer stock but will generally use InstiNet. Because the ECN order will be represented on the Level II screen, the trader is afforded limit-order protection, again meaning that a market maker will not be able to trade ahead of better (inside) orders. Therefore, if you want to buy and bid the highest for the stock, you want to buy before anyone else on the planet—including market makers. This is one of the keys to successful E-DAT trading.

The InstiNet Corporation is a privately operated, computerized system to facilitate fourth market trades (institution-to-institution direct trades) in both NASDAQ and listed securities. InstiNet was the first of all the ECNs and is still today the largest ECN by far. It is in a class by itself and deserves special attention. Institutional investors subscribing to the service can enter bids and offers and trade directly with other institutions. By special arrangement, individual traders can use the power of InstiNet to trade outside NASDAQ and the exchanges 24 hours a day, but actual liquidity is approximately 45 minutes before and after the NYSE hours. Only a top-quality broker-dealer can arrange this for you. It is one of the criteria you'll learn about later when I discuss the selection of an E-DAT brokerage firm in Chapter 11.

Keep in mind that listed stocks can trade on NASDAQ before and after market hours via InstiNet, but not during, due to a lack of liquidity (no market). Why trade a listed stock during market hours on NASDAQ when you can go to the exchange?

SCOPE OF THE REGIONAL EXCHANGES

I haven't mentioned the American Stock Exchange, nor the Boston, Philadelphia, Cincinnati, Chicago, or Pacific exchanges simply because the American will merge with NASDAQ and the other exchanges operate principally the same way as the NYSE. I also believe there will be more mergers between screen-based markets and traditional floor-based exchanges, but this is my opinion. The Pacific has made a wise choice by hosting OptiMark. Together they will make a considerable contribution to the overall liquidity available to traders of all sizes. You will be hearing a lot from this combination in the near future. Opti-Mark shows potential for being one of the most formidable systems available. In fact, the NASDAQ has tentative plans to use OptiMark as part of its system, which will be exciting to see.

ELECTRONIC SETTLEMENT

The National Clearing Corporation (NCC) acts for broker-dealers much the same way the Federal Reserve System acts for the banking industry. Securities transactions between broker-dealers are generally done through the Depository Trust Corporation (DTC). The DTC processes trades by computers to avoid the need to send the certificates to the firms to be later delivered to customers. Instead the cer-tificates trade in what is called a *street name,* and they are kept with the DTC in accounts that firms have with the DTC. This system is important for electronic traders who are then able to trade and sweep their money back to their accounts for the next trade within seconds!

Understanding these trading environments is the first key step to getting a picture of the markets in which you can electronically trade. Chapter 2 discusses how an electronic trader can make money in directional markets, both from the long and the short side, using the electronic "weapons systems" of execution, such as SuperDot, SOES, SelectNet, and ECNs. The rules associated with each of these systems will also be covered in more detail in Chapter 2, as well as the trading opportunities they offer.

CHAPTER **2**

TRADING RULES BECOME LAWS FOR TRUE E-DAT TRADERS

I often equate trading electronically with learning to fly a modern jet. The speed and power of electronic trading is just as impressive. Every move is magnified and you have the power to select the route you take to your destination. You can use a mandatory route that forces a market maker to immediately take your order, or you can place your bid or offer in the market to be matched or filled by a market maker or another investor through ECNs. Regular on-line trading does not offer this power and flexibility.

You command a system that flashes orders to the market so fast that even market orders are effective for momentum trading, which usually is not the case with normal on-line systems. Your poor counterparts—trying to trade through a traditional broker or even an on-line e-mail system—must filter their orders through their brokers, the trading desks, the clerks at the exchanges, etc. If they dare to use market orders, they have no idea what price they will get in fast markets. You, on the other hand, can be filled in seconds and limit slippage significantly.

This speed and power that gives E-DAT traders adrenaline rushes also demands higher levels of performance. There is little or no time to correct wrong moves. Your only consolation is that you can reverse your positions with the same speed that you got into them. Because of the power and speed you command, traditional traders' rules carry the weight of law for you. Put another way, the power is in "real time" and, therefore, not very forgiving. An example that comes to mind is that of a friend of mine who treated his execution system like a Windows program: His double click became a double buy. That is the power of E-DAT!

Before you despair, you should know that the better E-DAT trading software has the most important rules and safeguards built-in. For example, the software stops you from shorting the market on a downtick or accidentally overbuying or overselling stock. The good software functions as a traffic cop and keeps you out of trouble, so you can focus on what is important—trading.

It stands to reason that all the trading rules you would be required to follow when trading the traditional way, through a broker, must be adhered to when trading electronically, so some of the more important ones are reviewed in this section. As an E-DAT trader, you do not have a broker second-guessing you when you enter trades directly, so some of the rules governing order placement via electronic trading systems are discussed here. It is important to cover this material before we get into trading in Chapters 4 through 10.

LONG- AND SHORT-SALE RULES

You "go long" on stocks when you anticipate that prices will rise. You purchase the securities at a low price and sell them at a higher price. From your broker's perspective, these transactions result in "long sales" and you are afterwards considered "long the stocks." On the E-DAT trader's trading screen, the long-sale box is the default on most systems. It is only on short sales that you would have to indicate this type of trade by clicking on a box with the mouse.

It is critical that you know exactly which side of the market you are going to be on before you flash your order into the market. The speed at which you get filled sometimes does not allow second thoughts. If you do accidentally send an erroneous order—immediately attempt to cancel. If that is not possible, immediately close out the position. Do not wait to see how the trade comes out. You will only compound the error when you try to correct a trade you never planned on in the first place.

If you are typical, as a new trader you will probably trade the long side more often than the short side of the market. I really believe that at heart traders are all bulls. It is just more comforting to see stocks rise than fall. I have often told attendees at my seminars that if you cut open most traders' chests, you would probably find bull's horns coming out of both sides of their hearts.

As you get serious about E-DAT trading, you might want to give a little more thought to the bear in you because of the directional markets we see today. When you short a stock, you are anticipating that the stock you are trading will fall. Therefore, you borrow the stock from your broker to sell at the current price, which you feel is higher than it will be when you buy it back to cover your position. The DTC handles this automatically for you in day trading electronically when you simply click the short-sale function. With some firms, if you close out your position on the same day, you are not even charged any interest. If you think you might hold a short overnight, be sure to check with your broker-dealer to make sure there is stock to be borrowed. A good trading program will have the "short list" built in and let you download the stocks available off the Internet. Here are a few short-selling reminders:

- Short sales are always executed and accounted for in a customer's margin account and are subject to 50 percent initial margin requirements.
- Short sales are subject to higher NASD/NYSE minimum margin maintenance requirements than long purchases in a margin account. The maintenance margin is higher (30 percent) for short positions than for long positions (25 percent). If the short position goes beyond your maintenance requirement, your brokerage firm will take you out of the trade at a loss, so keep close track of your margin. Proper risk-management

skills should alleviate this risk inherently. If you get in a situation in which your electronic brokerage firm has to "buy you in" to avoid margin calls, you abandoned discipline and committed a cardinal sin of trading. More on this later in Chapter 6, but I like to take every chance to drive the need for discipline into the minds of traders!

- Short sales always entail the delivery of borrowed stock to the buy side because if you had the stock, you would be selling it instead of shorting. Since you do not have it, it must be borrowed.

- Not all stocks can be shorted. For example, a stock whose price is too low cannot be shorted. When no stock is available to be borrowed, it cannot of course be shorted. New issues cannot be shorted for the first 30 days of trading publicly.

- **Warning:** You can be "bought in" (your position can be closed out by the broker-dealer) at any time if the broker has to return the borrowed shares to the owner. This is mainly a danger with thinly traded stocks and hot new issues, after they have been public for over 30 days. For example, a hot new issue rises from $40 to $65 in one week and stalls. You short the stock and the next week the stock goes to $75. You realize you shorted too soon, but decide to hold your position anyway. While you are waiting for the price to fall, the owner of the shares you borrowed decides the stock has peaked and sells them. Your broker discovers that there are no more shares available in the market to borrow and is forced to close your position, at a $10-a-share loss to you. Your broker needs the shares to deliver them to the new owner at settlement. Generally, this is not a risk to the short-term, E-DAT trader, who covers trades intraday, but nevertheless it is a risk to be aware of.

- Because of the uptick rule, most shorts will be opened while selling into strength, meaning the stock will tend to move higher for a bit before it will reverse and turn downward. This creates more "heat" or negative pressure since you want the stock to fall so you can buy it back cheaper than you sold it. Your "risk elasticity" must be greater, therefore, when shorting. Selling stock "tops" is not realistic and the uptick rule requires you to sell into an advancing market.

EXCHANGE SHORT-SALE RULES

Orders to sell a listed security short on a listed exchange may be executed only on a "plus tick" or "zero-plus tick." A plus tick is a price higher than the last reported price. A zero-plus tick occurs when the last trade for the security was made at the same price as the trade before but *that* previous trade was higher than the previous trade (two trades ago). The plus tick or zero-plus tick carries over from the previous day's trading to the next day's opening.

OTC SHORT-SALE RULES

NASDAQ's short-sale rule prohibits member firms from entering short sales in its National Market System (NMS) for securities at or below the current inside bid whenever that bid is lower than the previous inside bid. An opening bid is a "down bid" if it is lower than the previous day's closing bid, or the same as the previous day's closing bid if that closing bid was a down bid.

This bid rule even includes bids that are canceled. For example, a market maker, let's say Goldman Sachs & Company (GSCO) has the high bid on a stock of 80. The bid/ask is 80 × 80⅛. Someone fires in a new bid of 80¹⁄₁₆ using Island, one of the ECNs. This is an uptick. Five seconds later, the 80¹⁄₁₆ bid is canceled. Goldman is still sitting there at 80. Even though no trades took place, this then becomes a downtick and cannot be shorted at the bid price.

In E-DAT, the brokerage firm that you have opened your trading account with is your agent, and the DTC provides the borrowed stock to cover day trades. Therefore, by clicking on the short-sell box on the order-execution screen, the uptick rule will be automatically tested for you. All you need to do is focus on which side of the market you wish to be trading. Professionally designed trading software will perform all the key functions (i.e., check the rules, identify the order as a long or a short, and borrow stock for short sales for intra-day trades).

TYPES OF ORDERS

Stocks, bonds, options, futures—securities of all types are all traded via highly sophisticated systems. Computerized routing and execution systems have revolutionized the way customer orders are handled. By using a computerized trading platform, you can trade at home or anywhere you can get on-line. This means you need a solid understanding of the various orders and how and when they will be filled. With a traditional on-line system you are given only two choices, market or limit orders. Because the dealers will want to make the spread, you will not be given the opprotunity to buy the bid (wholesale) and sell the offer (retail), which can only be facilitated through a SelectNet system or an ECN.

MARKET ORDERS

A market order is executed immediately at the price the market is trading. As long as the security is trading, a market order guarantees execution. It is the primary tool for high-velocity trading. No other type of order offers that guarantee. The disadvantage of a market order, in traditional trading, is that you do not know in advance the exact price you will receive. It is almost like giving your broker a blank check. You can experience slippage in price based on the liquidity and market volatility of the security being traded. This means the price you get could be higher or lower than the price of the security at the time you place your order. With a true E-DAT system, market orders make sense. Without direct access, it is very difficult to execute momentum trades.

Another electronic execution system available, but not offered on traditional on-line systems in addition to ECNs, is the SOES system. SOES allows you to get almost instantaneous fills when a market maker is on the inside market. I cannot emphasize enough how *powerful* this ability to get filled instantly is from the profit-taking and the risk-management perspectives. It tips the playing field in your favor. How would you like to be sitting out in the open, as a market maker does on the Level II screen, and have anyone in the world with a computer firing orders via a SOES gun at your bids and asks? In any high-velocity market, one with plenty of liquidity, you have the advantage, even over market makers, if you learn to use market orders effectively.

LIMIT ORDERS

The next class of orders is the limit orders, which are used primarily by the E-DAT trader to buy at the bid or sell at the ask through an ECN. They are called "limit orders" because they put a limit on the price at which your order can be filled.

Because limit orders put a restriction on the amount that can be paid or received for the securities, you may not get filled if the price limitation is not reached. Here are some examples:

- A sell limit sets a minimum price at which the owner of the stock is willing to sell. If a price of 102 is not achieved, no trade takes place in an order to "sell 1000 shares of IBM at 102 or better."
- A buy limit sets a maximum price at which the investor is willing to buy. If the price of 75 does not go down to the required level, no trade will be executed in an order to "buy 1000 shares of XON (Exxon) at 75 or better."
- Customers who enter limit orders risk missing the chance to buy or sell, especially if the market moves rapidly away from their limit. Chasing stock is a bad habit that is often seen in new E-DAT traders. By the time you catch up to the stock and get filled, you do not want it. Limit orders are great tools, but you need to use them properly!
- If a limit order is not executed, even if the limit price is reached, the explanation could be that there is "stock ahead" (i.e., another order at the same price took precedence). Think of it this way. You are number seven in line to buy a hot dog at the ball game. There are only five hot dogs left,

but you don't know that. The vendor says to the person in front of you, "Sorry, there are no more available." The vendor says this loud enough for you and the people behind you to hear it. That is what stock ahead is all about. The market has no more stock at that price available. If you placed a market order, you get the next best price, assuming you are the next in line. By then, the price could be many price levels away from where you thought it was. This is the primary downside to market orders as opposed to limit orders, and especially on an inferior system, such as most on-line systems. If it is a limit order, you simply do not get filled. Stock ahead is usually the reason. See Figure 2-1.

FIGURE 2-1   *Limit orders give you more control over the price at which you buy or sell securities.*

BLeSS and SLoBS are mnemonics to help keep stop orders straight:
1) **SL** - Sell Limit   2) **BS** - Buy Stop
SLoBS - Orders entered above CMV

CURRENT   MARKET

BLeSS - Orders entered below CMV
3) **BL** - Buy Limit   4) **SS** - Sell Stop

1)   Sell Limit orders are prices that represent the minimum a seller will accept. If a trader wants to protect a profit, he would use this order. Example, you buy at $25 and the stock is at $30 currently, you can add a sell limit order at $32 so that if it reaches this price you will be sold at this minimum price.
2)   Buy Stop orders are entered to buy the stock before it moves even higher.
3)   Buy Limit orders represent the maximum price to buy a stock. Enter this order if you want to buy stock but it is currently overvalued, and you want to buy the stock as it starts to fall lower to a more reasonable price.
4)   Sell Stops are placed to stop a decline and sell stock before it goes even lower. Use this order to protect a profit or limit a loss.

STOP ORDERS

A stop order is an order instructing the broker to enter a market order if the stock reaches the designated price, the stop or the trigger price. Like a rubber stop in a sink, once removed or triggered, things start to happen. Sell stop orders are made to protect profits and to stop losses. Sell stop orders are always entered at a price below the current offering price and are triggered when the market price touches or drops through the sell stop price. They protect investors' long positions in falling markets.

Buy stop orders are always entered at a price above the current offering price and are triggered when the market price touches or goes through the buy stop price. When the stop price is hit, the order becomes a market order and is immediately filled. Buy stop orders are usually made to limit the risk of short sales. They get the trader out of a upward moving market fast. Buy stops can also be used to get traders into long positions. For example, a trader may be waiting for a stock to make a new high before entering a long position. The buy stop would be set at the price of the new high, when hit or penetrated, the buy stop becomes a market order and is executed immediately before the stock continues higher.

STOP LIMIT ORDERS

Stop limit orders are a combination of the stop order and the limit order. The first step is the trigger or stop price. When the stop price is hit, the order becomes a regular limit order. For example, if you want to buy a stock when it penetrates an area of resistance at 60 by at least ⅛, you would place the following order: "Buy 1000 CSCO at a 60 stop, 60⅛ limit." A sell stop limit might read: "Sell 1000 CSCO at a 58 stop, limit 57½."

Think of stop limit orders as absentee management, since they provide management when a trader isn't around to put the order in if a price point is hit. But this is not the situation for most serious E-DAT traders. They are watching the market and monitoring all their positions. In most situations, there is no need for stop limit orders of any type for the true electronic trader. E-DAT traders use mental stops. They know what price they need to hit, and they watch for it. When the time and price to strike is met, they fire their electronic orders and are filled within seconds. Figure 2-1 will help you understand where stop orders are entered.

THE WEAPONS SYSTEM

If a market maker fails to honor a bid and ask for a specific number of shares, the market maker is said to be "backing away." The SOES system eliminates this possibility. When a trader initiates a SOES execution through a real-time system, the market maker is forced to buy or sell at least 200 shares at the price quoted on the system. In reality, quotes are in 1000-share increments, which is the maximum on SOES for any one trade.

When you use SOES, there are restrictions, and these rules are built into all quality trading platforms:

1. SOES trades are executed in share lots of 1000 shares or less.
2. The "five-minute rule" prohibits a trader from executing a trade on the same side for a security within five minutes. For example, a trader who buys 1000 shares of DELL using SOES must wait five minutes before purchasing DELL again using the SOES system. The five-minute rule also prevents a trader from reversing a position. For example, a trader who buys 1000 shares of DELL and then closes this position by selling the shares using the SOES system, must wait five minutes after this sale to sell the stock short using the SOES system. This restriction does not apply to trades executed using non-mandatory systems, such as SelectNet and ECNs (InstiNet, Island, Archipelago, Attain, RediBook, and Bloomberg).
3. Registered reps or members of broker dealers cannot trade SOES for their own account—another plus for a more level playing field for the individual trader.
4. You cannot enter a SOES trade in any stock in which the firm with whom you have your account with makes a market.

5. Selling short on SOES may not be done on a downtick. A downtick, as defined by NASDAQ, means the current bid is lower than the previous bid. The simplest way to tell if you can short a stock, is to check the direction of the arrow next to the bid on market maker screens of most E-DAT software or on Level II screens provided by a real-time system. If there is a red down arrow, you cannot short the stock at or below the current bid. But you can short a stock in this situation if you offer the stock on a nonmandatory system such as SelectNet, and ECNs, such as Island or InstiNet at a price above the current bid.

This rule exists to retard the descent of a stock if it is beginning to fall. Longs are permitted to sell, but disallowing new short positions often helps control or slow down a selling frenzy.

6. SOES trading is a mandatory execution system, as mentioned earlier. A market maker must trade at least the number of shares posted at the price advertised. On most NASDAQ stocks the number of shares quoted is 1000. However, other situations dictate 200- and 500-share requirements. The market maker is only required to trade at his posted level once. The market maker then has 15 seconds to either refresh the bid or offer or pull it. See Figure 2-2.

SELECTNET/ECNs

Nonmandatory systems operate differently than SOES, in that they are completely voluntary on both sides of the transactions. SelectNet is a system sponsored by NASDAQ and widely used by both market makers and traders. You can enter your order as a bid to buy a certain number of shares (not limited to 1000) at a certain price or as an offer to sell a certain number of shares at a specified price. The market maker may hit your bid or lift your offer to trigger an execution. SelectNet bids and offers do not appear on the Level II market maker screen. Only market makers and NASDAQ workstation subscribers see SelectNet bids and offers.

FIGURE 2-2   *The Small Order Execution System (SOES) is one of the ways you can route your buy and sell orders directly to NASDAQ. It is a very powerful trading tool.*

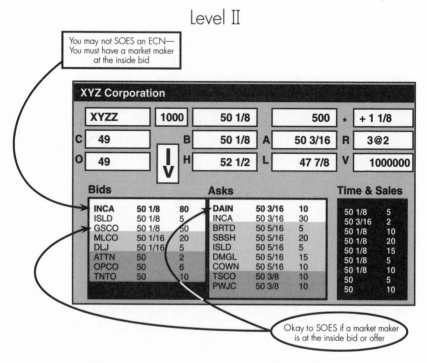

Okay to SOES if a market maker is at the inside bid or offer

The SelectNet system eliminated the need for market makers to call each other by telephone. Bids and offers can be broadcast to all subscribers and executed via electronic means. An advantage of SelectNet, other than the possibility to buy between the spread, is its ability to hide your intentions from other traders. However, I do not feel the volume traded by E-DAT will affect the market to the point where this is ever a concern, unless you are trading illiquid stocks, which I feel is a big mistake.

For example, if you know that GSCO (Goldman Sachs) is a buyer of stock you own and you wish to sell it to GSCO, you can use a "Preference Feature." This feature allows you to send the order directly and only to GSCO. If GSCO is willing to pay higher than the current high bid price, but does not want to show other traders it is bidding high on the Level II screen, Goldman may buy your stock above the current bid on SelectNet. You get a better fill and Goldman gets the stock it wants without showing its hand by joining the high bids. If you do not specify the preference feature, your order is broadcast to all subscribers or market makers. Remember, SelectNet is like calling GSCO on the phone and asking if it wants to buy at your sell price or vice versa.

You, as an individual trader, do not have to worry about showing weakness in a market when you route your order through an ECN because there is so much volume these days. Strength or weakness is revealed only when the market maker buys above the market or repeatedly buys without changing its bid. That is why Goldman would route the order through SelectNet. If Goldman continued to buy or bid for stock—without changing its bid—on the Level II screen, every savvy trader in that market would spot it in a "New York minute," realizing GSCO had an order to fill and was a net buyer versus a net seller, and go long to try to "front run" its big order.

The term *front running* means trading ahead of someone else. Registered representatives, or brokers, are prohibited from front running their customers. This means, if they have a client that places a large order that will give the market a jolt, they cannot place an order for their own account before the client's order to take advantage of the impact of the customer's order. The front-running regulation does not apply in this circumstance because, as an E-DAT trader, you do not have any proprietary information or tools that give you an unfair advantage. Your trained eye to suspect what is happening on Level II is a huge advantage and very legitimate.

If a broker front runs an order it is illegal, because the order is given to the broker by a customer who expects confidentiality. For example, you are a new broker, like Charlie Sheen in *Wall Street,* and Gordon Gecko calls with an order for 500,000 shares of Big Blue (IBM). Charlie says to himself, Gordon must know something so I'll buy some too. This is illegal because Chuck broke a rule as a broker. He is using proprietary, confidential information for his own good (forget the rest of the movie because Gordon was pond scum, but I wanted to use this familiar movie to make this single point). No such rule exists for an E-DAT trader who has the same tools as anyone else who can read the tape well enough to think GSCO is buying and staying at the bid for a reason. The E-DAT trader doesn't know that there is a buy order, but feels there is one, based on GSCO's buying appetite. This is completely acceptable and what an E-DAT trader should be focusing on.

The primary difference between SOES and SelectNet is that a SOES trade is initiated by an individual trading at a market maker's advertised price, while a SelectNet trade is initiated by the market maker trading with the electronic trader. SelectNet trades are referred to as nonmandatory, because traders are bidding or offering the stock to the market maker at a specified price. Thus, the market maker must "elect" to execute the order for the trade to be consummated. The market maker is not obligated to execute a SelectNet bid or offer. Conversely, with SOES the market maker is traded to or hit because it is mandatory.

InstiNet is an ECN primarily used by mutual, pension, and hedge funds and other large institutions. InstiNet accounts for a very large percentage of all shares traded on NASDAQ, and it is important to be aware of InstiNet's position at all times. It is the oldest and largest of the ECNs. The better electronic brokerage firms can get access to InstiNet for their retail customers.

ECNs

You cannot execute a SOES order against any of the nonmandatory systems. If you enter a SOES market or limit order to buy or sell a stock when there are only ECNs at the inside, your order will be kicked out with the error message "No SOES market maker available." If you have an active SOES order entered at a time when the last registered market maker leaves that price level, and the Level II screen shows an ECN still at that level, you will be kicked out in a similar fashion.

This occurs because market makers are the only participants required by NASD regulations to honor a two-sided market. ECNs are broker-dealers, but not market makers. An ECN allows you to trade directly with other customers without a market maker in between to make a profit from both traders. Think of ECNs as crossing networks, matching buyers with sellers.

Most ECNs do not sell their order flow. They will match buyers with sellers without marking up the stock (without a spread), unlike the situation that exists with on-line systems that sell their order flow to wholesalers who make the spread and cost unsuspecting investors billions of dollars a year as an industry.

As a brief look in the future, I believe ECNs and market makers will be treated the same way, by this I mean ECNs will also be required to honor their quotes through a mandatory system. Proposed changes like these can be viewed at the NASD Web site at **www.nasdaqtrader.com.** Whatever rules and system changes occur, the future is very bright for the general public to compete on equal footing with the industry professionals. In fact, the individual trader has a distinct advantage because who cares more about your money than you? Market makers are not trading their own money; it is the firm's money they work for. Market makers are just people like you. Since it is not their capital at risk, they won't trade it with the care with which you will trade your money.

THE SUPERDOT SYSTEM

Let's go into a little more depth regarding the SuperDot system, which, as I mentioned earlier, is an electronic order-routing system that enables member firms to quickly and efficiently transmit market and limit orders in all NYSE-listed securities. The orders are sent directly to the specialist's post or to the member firm's booth where they are executed in the auction market. A report of executions is returned to the member firm's office over the same electronic circuit that brought the order to the trading floor. The execution is then submitted to the consolidated tape-reporting system. The SuperDot system routes to the NYSE and AMEX only. Think of SuperDot as your electronic floor broker on these exchanges. This system truly creates a virtual execution system on Wall Street, USA.

THE DISPLAY BOOK (ELECTRONIC BOOK)

At the trading post, SuperDot orders that come in from member firm systems appear on the specialist's Display Book screen. The Display Book is an electronic workstation that keeps track of all limit orders and incoming market orders.

Various Windows-like screen applications allow the specialist to view one or more issues at a time at various levels of detail. Incoming SuperDot limit orders automatically enter the Display Book. The Display Book sorts the limit orders and displays them in price/time priority.

When a floor broker gives the specialist a limit order, the specialist's clerk enters the order into the Display Book. SuperDot market orders are displayed at the terminal and await further action. The order execution may be against another order on the book, against the specialist's inventory, or against an order represented by a floor broker in "the crowd." *The crowd* is composed of the floor traders around the specialist with orders to buy and/or sell that specialist's stock.

The message that an order has been executed (in part or whole) is called a *report*. The report goes from the specialist, via SuperDot, to the Consolidated Quotation System (CQS) and the member who entered the order. Trades involving more than one SuperDot order will generate more than one report. The ultimate destination of the execution report is the person or entity that placed the order, you the E-DAT trader.

OPTIMARK—THE NEWEST ELECTRONIC TRADING SYSTEM

From the examples in this chapter, you should have learned two things. When a major trader, be it a market maker, institution or even a mutual fund, has a large amount of stock to sell or buy, it can move the market. If you detect that move, you can profit by shadowing their trading. The second thing you have learned is that market makers go to great lengths to hide their intentions in hopes of completing the trade before the market is run up or down on them, which would generate a market impact cost, or MIC.

A new electronic trading system, called OptiMark, will make it easier to hide these giant trades, or large institutional orders. Oddly enough, OptiMark offers an important benefit to the average trader by giving those who are trading 1000 or more shares, a very good chance at "price improvement." Price improvement is an industry term that simply means you get a better average price for your stock than you would normally expect, or an improved price over or under your limit price. Because large institutions will see this system as a means of anonymously representing their orders, the liquidity Opti-Mark will attract will be incredible.

Price improvement for the average trader can occur because OptiMark aggregates virtually the entire stock market. It aggregates the fragmented market where the same stock is being traded on more than one exchange. The liquidity of the retail market can be combined with the institutional to give all traders more liquidity and anonymity. That is the objective of OptiMark. With that increased anonymity, small E-DAT's like us will be able to share in price improvement.

Your order, when traded on OptiMark, can be electronically presented to pension funds, mutual funds, and other major players. The larger traders are attracted to OptiMark because they can trade anonymously, hiding their intentions with the hope of not unduly running up or down the price of the stock they are trading. More importantly, OptiMark is designed to allow them to create a wide array of strategies. When trading a large block, say 500,000 shares, the portfolio manager may be willing to sell portions of the block at different prices, as long as the average price is within an acceptable range. This is where the small trader can get a break or some price improvement. For example, the portfolio manager might be willing to sell the majority at or within ⅛ or the current bid and the rest at ¼ to ½ off the bid. This order is cycled into the entire pool of orders from all the exchanges, along with yours. You might well come out of the order-matching process with an extra ⅛ to ¼. In fact, it would make sense to place your bid below the current market value first to try and price improve.

Needless to say, I am very enthusatic about OptiMark and the positive potential it has to add an enormous amount of liquidity to the markets. Once it is approved and implemented you must have an account with a brokerage firm that is certified to trade on OptiMark or one that has access to it via some other arrangement.

By now, you should be getting a feel for how direct access electronic trading works. You can take advantage of the E-DAT systems to substantially improve your trading skills and returns. E-DAT is the future. Speaking of the future, let's now move to Chapter 3 on the "futures" market and how it can be a leading indicator to stock price movement.

CHAPTER 3

NAVIGATIONAL AIDS FOR TRADING IN THE VIRTUAL STOCK MARKET

Flying an airplane and trading electronically are both extremely fast-moving activities, laced with a certain amount of risk. These skills call for split-minute decision making and require a substantial amount of training. Both depend heavily on in-depth training on a simulator before soloing. A key subject in any ground school is navigation.

For the trader, navigation means knowing the direction the market is trending. The primary navigational tools are the various stock indexes. But most indexes are lagging indicators. They tell us where the market has been, rather than where it is headed. That is why I recommend that you use the S&P 500 Futures and the 30-Year Bond Futures as your navigational beacons, since they are leading indicators.

THE S&P 500 INDEX AND FUTURES CONTRACT

Let's begin our discussion with the actual S&P 500 (cash stocks) and then we will talk about its derivative, the futures contract. The S&P 500 is primarily made up of large capitalization stocks of the NYSE, and does contain NASDAQ stocks as well. Because of this fact, the NYSE is most affected by futures trading. The S&P 500 is the benchmark for most mutual funds. Almost every fund manager is interested in beating this index since this benchmark is what defines their ability to manage a stock mutual fund.

Why is the S&P 500 such an important index? The answer can be found in the word "disintermediation." This pertains to a recent phenomenon when, for the first time in the history of the United States, security deposits exceeded bank deposits. The cause is the baby boomers and the way they invest. People are bullish on the stock market. Mutual funds are the most common investment for the vast majority of Americans who do not have the confidence or the desire to trade their own portfolios. Baby boomers have led this charge to mutual funds and therefore have changed the stock market and the way people think of the market. The culture has changed forever, through baby boomers' children, and even their own parents.

Because so much money pours into mutual funds and the S&P 500 is the benchmark of the fund managers, this index is by far the best gauge of market direction and sentiment. Keep in mind this index, like all indices, is not a leading indicator or even a coincident indicator—but a lagging indicator, or barometer, of what has happened.

So why do we, as traders who want to predict stock movement, care so much about the S&P 500? Because the derivative counterpart market of the S&P 500, the S&P 500 Futures Contract, trades against it in an inverse relationship and is a leading indicator. The futures or financial futures market is the most efficient market for fund managers to put huge assets to work in the shortest time. (Can you believe that it is harder to keep $500 million working and performing than $10 million!) These managers need fast, efficient ways to keep the flood of money coming into the market productive. Therefore, let's take a quick look at the futures market and how you can use it in your trading.

Futures, in my opinion, are the most accurate indication for short-term strategies because so much of the sentiment in stock is reflected there first. Part of this is because the S&P 500 is a key benchmark for mutual fund managers, but also because it is so actively traded by fund managers and institutions. As a result of all the dollars being thrown at these two markets, an arbitrage opportunity has been created. For example, if futures trade "rich," they will be sold to buy the underlying stocks. Or if the futures trade "lean," the underlying stocks will be sold to buy the undervalued futures. This arbitrage situation can be used as a leading indicator by the short-term trader. As this shift of money occurs, the money flow of mutual funds and institutions are one of the most accurate indicators available, and the futures market can be a good barometer of that flow.

Fair Value, available on CNBC each morning, reflects the mathematical relationship between the S&P Futures Contract and the S&P 500 or actual underlying stock known as the "cash."

Fair Value is strictly a technical equation which measures the benefit of owning the actual stock itself of the S&P 500 or its derivative counterpart, the futures contracts.

Financial futures are bets of where a basket of stocks will be in terms of price at a specific date in the future. Like an option, one party buys a contract and the other sells. At the expiration of the contract, buyer and seller make or lose the difference between what the underlying S&P 500 basket of stock is worth versus what they bought or sold it for. Financial futures are called derivatives because they are derived from the actual underlying stock.

It is important to mention that more money is lost by average traders and investors in the derivative markets, such as options and futures, than the actual equities market for some reasons worth mentioning; equities truely create value, while derivatives are simply a "zero-sum game."

Because stocks do have intrinsic value and are tangible assets, there will be more bias to them than products like options and futures, which will always expire. Smart traders will therefore be more attracted to tangible assets like stock. Understanding this, it makes sense that stock ownership is more expensive and requires more capital. Therefore many undercapitalized investors who pose

the deadly traits of greed and fear will flock to markets they have little business being in, e.g., derivatives. The twin attraction of small
capital outlay to buy options and the fear of buying expensive stock
has placed more "dumb money" in these markets than any other time
in history. This is why many small investors lose so much money in
derivative markets.

This is important because the futures market will tend to attract
much attention by fund managers, but only for short periods of time.
Principally because well-capitalized institutions like funds will gravi-
tate to tangible equity securities, and hold positions longer because
of the tangibility compared to derivatives, which will expire like any
commodity, such as oranges.

As we examine Fair Value and the relationship it has to futures,
keep these facts in mind. These are some of the reasons why the
indications produced by futures are so short-lived.

The S&P 500 Futures Contract trades on the Chicago Mercantile
Exchange, completely independent of the S&P itself. The contracts
expire quarterly. When you see the Fair Value screen on CNBC, it is
always the most current contract, the one closest to expiration. It is
referred to as the "front month." So, in late December, after the
December contract expires, the front month is the March contract. A
day before the March contract expires, June becomes the front
month, and so on. You can get more information on futures contracts
from the Chicago Mercantile Exchange Web site (see Appendix C).

These contracts almost always trade higher than where the S&P
500 index is, because most people assume stocks will rise over time.
The difference between the two, the futures and the cash itself is
called the *spread,* or the *premium,* since the futures are usually at a
premium to cash. For example,

S&P Futures is at 1015.00

S&P 500 (Cash) is at 1010.00

Here the spread or premium is five points, or 5.00. You can find
this on CNBC and good E-DAT systems.

FAIR VALUE

When the spread is at Fair Value, it makes no economic difference to own the futures or the actual stocks. I consider this to be muted information. But when the spread drops below Fair Value or moves above it by a large enough margin, then one of the choices, stocks or futures, become more attractive. Arbitrageurs sell one and buy the other to capture the spread.

The spread or premium changes throughout the day because the futures contract and the actual S&P 500 trade independently. Supply and demand in the futures trading pit in Chicago determines the price of the futures contract. The cumulative supply and demand for all 500 stocks determines the S&P 500. Sometimes these forces go in opposite directions, or they go in the same direction at different speeds. When that happens, the spread changes.

Assume for this example that on a given morning the Fair Value looks like this:

Spread	5.00
BUY	6.00
Fair Value	5.00
SELL	4.00

Here is how you would interpret this information before the stock market opens:

- The front month S&P 500 futures contract closed last night 5.00 higher than the actual S&P 500 index for a spread or premium of 5.00.
- Fair Value for that day is also 5.00. Fair Value does not change during the day. However, as each day passes, it gets a little smaller, because the time left until futures expiration is part of the value, known as *time value*.

- Buy programs are likely to be triggered if or when the spread widens to 6.00.
- Sell programs should be expected to hit stocks if or when the spread narrows to 4.00.

It is like reading weather information in your flight plan telling you when you *might* meet some turbulence in your flight. As the spread widens or contracts, the astute E-DAT trader evaluates this information to enter, maintain, or exit trades.

Here is how you can use it in your trading. Assume the market opens with the spread at Fair Value. But as trading begins, the futures and the cash go their separate ways. If the spread widens to 6.00, the institutions will find stocks more attractive to own than the futures contract. So, they buy stocks and sell the futures. If the spread narrows to 4.00, the institutions sell stocks and buy futures. So by monitoring the spread, one can get a good idea of whether to expect sudden selling or buying by the institutions.

The act of selling tends to depress price, while buying tends to raise price. So, the programs that the institutions trigger tend to drive the spread back to Fair Value very quickly. With a wide spread between the futures and the cash (futures are too expensive relative to Fair Value), buying stocks and selling futures drives the cash index up and the futures down, which narrows the spread, returning it to Fair Value. Therefore, the impact on the market from hitting these buy and sell levels can be very short-lived. As you will learn later, your ability to execute trades in seconds gives you the opportunity to capture the moves generated by program trading (described in the next section).

PROGRAM TRADING

An active member of my trading business, Kevin Ward, has shared his thoughts on program trading, which truly filters into usable strategy regarding futures. His thoughts here are important. Kevin traded in Chicago on the Merchantile Exchange for several years.

If you are not familiar with program trading, let me clarify it and bring this often misunderstood professional trading tool into the realm of the short-term electronic trader.

The Big Board defines program trading as the simultaneous buying or selling of at least 15 different stocks with a market value of $1 million or more. The exchange accommodates program trading through the SuperDot system, which distributes buy and sell orders to exchange-floor specialist posts.

A program is run with a simple touch of a button. A buy program occurs when stocks are bought and futures are instantly sold. Conversely, a sell program is initiated when stocks are sold and futures are instantly bought.

In index arbitrage, the price of the S&P 500 (cash stocks) in New York is constantly compared with the S&P Futures Contract traded in Chicago. To profit from an index arbitrage opportunity, the arbitrage firm that owns the S&P 500 in New York must sell it and replace it with a cheaper S&P 500 Futures Contract from the Chicago Mercantile Exchange.

Institutional investors, retail brokerage houses, and private corporations all may participate in program trading. Institutional investors, who dominate the markets, spend much of their time gathering, digesting, and acting on information with the aid of sophisticated computer programs. They are constantly reevaluating stocks, bonds, real estate, and the derivative markets in the light of new information. When a development occurs anywhere in the world that significantly changes the value of an investment, a trading decision can be made quickly either to buy or sell.

Program trading offers a low-cost way to manage big stock portfolios. By most accounts, computerized trading results in lower transaction costs. Also, program trading acts as a profit center for brokerage houses, allowing them to offer another service to institutional clients.

Executing transactions with lightning speed, program trading has quickened Wall Street's reaction to news. In turn, stock prices better reflect market forces, with increased price and volume changes. Pure index arbitrage accounts for nearly half of current program trading. Program trading generally accounts for 17 to 22 percent of the daily NYSE volume.

Program trades may significantly and dramatically affect the overall market direction for as little as a few minutes to possibly as long as 60 or 70 minutes, depending on the size and frequency of the basket (the number) of stocks and overall dollar value. It is not uncommon for a program trade to move the DJIA 30 to 40 points. The *Wall Street Journal* reports the weekly activity of program trading and the percentage of the overall NYSE volume.

There are some occasions when the futures and cash remain out of equilibrium. The futures may continue to trade at a level significantly above or significantly below Fair Value. NYSE Rule 80-A prohibits index arbitrage when the Dow's net change for the day exceeds 50 points or when the Dow's net change for the day has fallen by greater than 50 points. Consequently, program traders are unable to execute and eliminate the unbalanced market. You may find a strong move up, in which the futures continue to trade at a level above where buy programs should be triggered, but because of Rule 80-A, programs cannot be executed.

When the Dow falls to a level below positive 25 or has rallied to a level greater than negative 25, Rule 80-A is no longer in effect. Rule 80-A is commonly referred to as the NYSE *trading curb.*

How does program trading affect short-term electronic trading? Fundamentally, three situations have to be addressed in E-DAT:

- Trade entry
- Trade maintenance
- Trade exiting

Obviously, all traders hope to initiate trades that immediately move in their favor. However, several times there are pull-back periods until you can realize a profit. With careful observation of when program trades kick in (reported by CNBC throughout the day), you may reduce the time lag in entering a trade.

For example, as the offer side begins to trade more rapidly and the size of the bid begins to grow, you must have an idea of whether buy programs or sell program levels are within realistic reach. Also, you must know whether Rule 80-A (NYSE curbs) are in effect. If programs are initiated, you may want to trade a moment sooner than usual because of the market-moving impact of the program trading activity. Traders may be more inclined to give up the edge or spread in this example and lift an offer (buy the offer) because of the potential impact of buy programs. Realistically, not all programs are going to have a significant market impact but having a feel for their ability to cause short-term volatility can lead to greater confidence when entering a trade.

Once in a trade, it is still as important to be aware of program activity. If hopes are realized, programs will continue in the direction of your position and you will be able to benefit from a wave of one-sided market movement. With some cushion in a trade (a trade in the money) and all other things being equal, you may tend to hold onto a long position a second longer if buy program levels are within reach.

However, if you wait until programs have completely run their course, it becomes too late to patiently work the offer side of the market. The market exhausts itself and turns in the opposite direction. One should get out at the bid immediately. Generally, markets that hold premium, that is, trade at levels significantly above Fair Value, are considered positive and more bullish. A negative or bearish tone is generally associated with markets that consistently trade below Fair Value.

Monitoring the futures/cash differential throughout the day may help one to confirm or deny overall market strength or weakness and consequently determine whether an existing position still warrants being open.

Continuing with the general buy program example (long-side position) and knowing whether buy program levels are within reach, you are afforded the opportunity to exit your position by working the offer and being a bit more patient. This can be justified when you have the feel for the impact of a buy program. Conversely, the opportunity to "squeeze" your position can also be justified when there is a program trade going the other way. Therefore, you may want to aggressively hit a bid and immediately exit a long position because of impending program trades.

Only with critical day-to-day observations and focus do you develop the skill to spot movements in the S&P 500 cash and subsequent activity in the S&P 500 futures that alerts you to program trading activity. Those who put the effort in to understand this professional trading method and incorporate it into their personal trading style will be solidifying their base of trading skills. Linked with activity shown on the Level II market maker screen and price ticker, you will be assembling the tools needed for trading confidently and profitably.

BOND FUTURES AND THE BUSINESS CYCLE: OTHER KEY INDICATORS

One of the few other indicators you should review daily, with as much attention as the S&P futures, are the bond futures and yield curve. These tend to be the best indicators of interest rate changes. When bond yields fall, bond and stock prices rise.

Good things happen to the stock market when the cost of money is cheap. Corporations expand. Demand for goods and services increase, since the consumer can borrow cheaper to buy that new car, vacation home, etc. While this is positive for the markets as it happens, it can have a negative effect as inflation and bond yields rise, hence increasing the cost of money and tightening of the money supply. This drives consumer spending down, forcing earnings and revenues lower for businesses. Eventually the stock markets and futures markets "tank."

The market reflects the general economy or business cycle, which sets the long-term tone of the stock market. The business cycle is composed of four phases:

- *Expansion or recovery phase*. This phase is characterized by marked increases in business activity.
- *Peak*. As business activities expand, employment and incomes rise. When full or near-full employment is achieved

and incomes are at or near highs, it is considered a period of prosperity.

- *Contraction.* Following a peak there is a period of contraction. Mild short-term contractions, lasting two or three quarters, are known as recessions. More severe and longer-term contractions are deemed depressions.
- *Trough.* At the bottom of the trough business activity appears to have come to a complete standstill. Eventually, the long climb up begins. As the ascent picks up the pace, it turns into a period of expansion.

The total annual output of a country (goods and services) is known as the gross domestic product (GDP). In periods of depression, the GDP decreases. In periods of expansion, it grows. It is important to be aware of the business cycle phase and its impact on the overall trend of the stock market. See Figure 3-1.

FIGURE 3-1   *The Business Cycle is the overall trend maker of the stock market. If the economy is strong, so is the stock market. If the country is in recession, it is felt in the markets.*

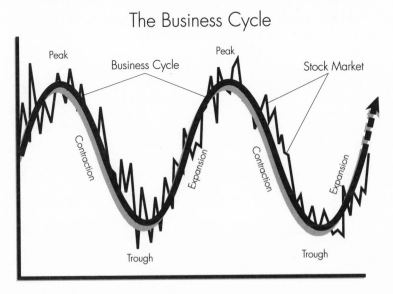

The Business Cycle

Having a broad, or "macro," perspective of the market is important, just as a "micro" view is. In order for someone to trade equities, futures, bonds, and the business cycle are all good navigational beacons to tune into. As we enter the next chapter on technical analysis, we will take a more macro look at individual stock analysis from a technician's perspective. Balancing common sense on what is happening around you in the economy with some of the technical tools E-DAT offers is the balance you want to begin your trading experience.

We have taken a good look at some micro economic indicators, such as the S&P futures and tick indicator, both of which help find short-term price change. Technical analysis, on the other hand, is a bit more broad-based and offers trading opportunities for longer time horizons, such as one to five days. Many "investors" laugh when they hear me talk about one to five days as a longer time horizon, but to E-DAT traders, it really is.

CHAPTER 4

UNDERSTANDING TECHNICAL ANALYSIS KEEPS YOU FLYING HIGH

If aviation students don't learn how to avoid severe weather conditions, they are not going to be flying long. The same is true for E-DAT traders. Technical analysis provides you with insights into stock price patterns that can predict what other traders are going to do, so you can take advantage of them or avoid them—just as aviators must learn how to use or dodge certain meteorological events.

The subject of technical analysis covers a vast spectrum of approaches to forecasting price movements. It ranges from drawing simple trend lines on price charts to elaborate computer programs attempting to emulate price activity to reading tea leaves. Its importance lies in the acceptance that past price patterns repeat. This belief, in turn, evolves from the realization that technical analysis objectively reveals the psychology of all traders in the market at a given time. Additionally, due to its wide acceptance, it often becomes a self-fulfilling prophecy. If enough traders see the same pattern and interpret it identically, enough of them act the same, either buying or selling the stock, to make the pattern reliable enough for you to trade successfully. This phenomenon often occurs with the simpler chart formations.

Due to the depth of the material on technical analysis, I am only going to deal in this text with those particular studies that have merit, in my opinion, for the E-DAT trader. If you wish to pursue the subject in greater detail, there are many, many excellent books available on the subject that will take you as deep as you would ever want to go. Mostly I feel the value of technical analysis lies in the theory that the psychology of market can be modeled in the charts. This psychology manifests itself in price patterns, which reflect human behavior. Others will use complicated theories, such as Fibonacci, chaos, or the movements of Venus and Mars to predict the next market boom or bust. "Paralysis from analysis" comes to mind when I think of the traders who subscribe to these theories, but many disagree. Here lies another wonderful common denominator of the market—there seems to be as many trading styles as there are personalities, and this, in my opinion, is the single most attractive characteristic of trading. Whether you are a Harvard graduate, high school dropout, male or female, young or old, intuitive and "street smart" or logical and precise, trading has a place for all souls who aspire to it.

I will begin this discussion by identifying where to find the stocks that lend themselves best to successfully using technical analysis (TA). You might do well to begin by trading stocks in the follow categories and time horizons:

- NASDAQ stocks
- Specifically the technology sector of NASDAQ
- Over one- to five-day time periods

NASDAQ stock performance conforms to what is expected from active growth companies. TA is used more in the tech stock sector than in any other sector and with the greatest degree of accuracy, in my opinion. I think it is undeniable that many have found success in this sector using technical indications.

The foundation of TA is charting (see Figure 4-1). Charts provide 20/20 hindsight and are not leading indicators. So why is this approach so widely accepted in the trading community? The answer

FIGURE 4-1   *Price charts are graphic representations of a stock's price history. They can cover any time horizon you are trading, from minutes to months. Volume (number of shares traded) depicts activity, and volatility measures the price stability.*

Price, Volume, and Volatility Chart

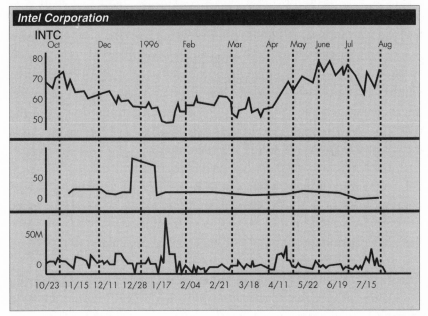

is based on trend extension. TA is built on the premise that events and behavioral patterns can be charted and can be expected to repeat. This is the theory, but not always reality.

In fact, to help identify criminal types and to treat mental illness, psychologists profile people by charting behavior. Their objective is to prevent violent acts from happening and to predict destructive behavior before it happens. This concept of charting behavior is the very foundation of TA. People (traders are people) control the markets and react to them in such a way that behavioral patterns can be recognized, measured, and predicted. This procedure does not predict earnings or the next stock split, but it does key in on the perception and, more importantly, the reaction elicited by these types of events.

By charting price activity to news-driven events, you can spot overreactions and predict that the same reaction will probably occur again. For example, when Dell moves 20 points after the announcement of a split, it can be predicted that many speculators will trade the next split announcement similarly. The problem is that in time the effect becomes well known and the reaction becomes sewed or less reliable because traders expect a certain reaction. As more people anticipate that reaction, the reaction becomes less accurate. This is the dynamics of TA and why it seems to be a short-lived event when a pattern is recognized. The trading community picks up on the expected reaction and by trading to that reaction, it destroys the outcome. As a result, TA is always changing. It is the most dynamic trading discipline there is and therefore requires the most work.

For the same reasons that psychologists want their patients to talk to them in order to understand their behavior, technical analysts need movement from stocks to chart their behavioral patterns. Since the NASDAQ and the tech sector, in particular, have been so active, they have become the focus of much technical analysis. Simply put, this sector has produced more data than any other and, therefore, lends itself to more analysis and attention.

Here are the technical indicators the E-DAT trader needs to monitor. This is only a small portion of technical analysis, but these indicators are, in my opinion, the most useful for you, as an E-DAT trader:

- Resistance and support lines
- Volume
- Angle of attack
- Advance and decline lines

RESISTANCE AND SUPPORT

Resistance and support levels of stock are the most well received indicators in charting stocks because so many professional traders and institutions look at these as viable analytic tools. When a breakout or breakdown occurs, because it is viewed by so many, it tends to gain strength because so much money flows in the direction of the trend. It, in effect, creates a self-fulfilling prophecy. See Figure 4-2.

Another barometer for the technician is ADX, a measurement of trend strength. It is a complicated mathematical formula that produces a value for what are called *directional indicators* or DIs. A "+DI" is a positive movement to the upside and, of course, a "−DI" is negative. When ADX is present, it indicates a trend. The DI measures the strength of the trend. Software programs can be purchased to calculate ADX, such as Trade Station, Advanced Get, and Real Tick III.

Resistance lines are lines drawn on price charts at levels that stocks have trouble penetrating. They seem to put lids on a stock's

---

FIGURE 4-2   *Traders carefully watch the price levels that slow down or halt a stock's price advance (resistance) or decline (support). These are vital clues as to when to buy or sell a stock.*

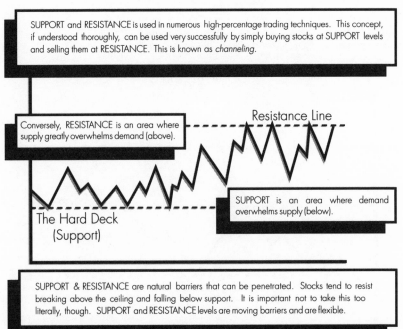

Support and Resistance

SUPPORT and RESISTANCE is used in numerous high-percentage trading techniques. This concept, if understood thoroughly, can be used very successfully by simply buying stocks at SUPPORT levels and selling them at RESISTANCE. This is known as *channeling.*

Conversely, RESISTANCE is an area where supply greatly overwhelms demand (above).

Resistance Line

SUPPORT is an area where demand overwhelms supply (below).

The Hard Deck (Support)

SUPPORT & RESISTANCE are natural barriers that can be penetrated. Stocks tend to resist breaking above the ceiling and falling below support. It is important not to take this too literally, though. SUPPORT and RESISTANCE levels are moving barriers and are flexible.

upward movement because the perceptions associated with these levels are outside the trading community's belief of where this stock should trade. Think of resistance lines as imaginary rubber ceilings that will flex and give a bit, but once penetrated will allow stocks to soar. A lot of pent-up energy is released (see the Sonic Boom in Figure 4-3).

Support lines are imaginary lines that prop up stocks when prices reach these levels. Stocks resist going any lower than these price points. Once broken, the stocks seem to crash fast, as all the confined downward pressure is released (see the Crash Landings in Figure 4-4).

The support and resistance lines or levels are, once again, imaginary lines that suggest prices in any given stock that resist penetration. The TradeWise software, Trade Station, Advanced Get, and Real Tick III are examples of computer platforms that allow you to plot these levels in any time frame. If you are trading intraday, you might plot support/resistance lines using one-hour intervals. Or you could

FIGURE 4-3 *Sonic Booms are chart formations that signal traders that stocks are about to make significant moves to higher ground.*

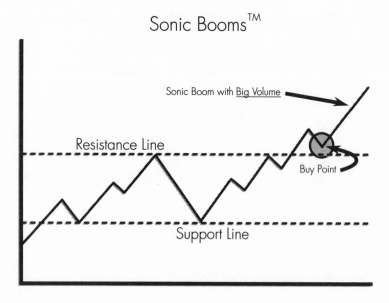

FIGURE 4-4 *Crash Landings are the opposite of Sonic Booms. They signal opportunities for short stock plays to the savvy investor.*

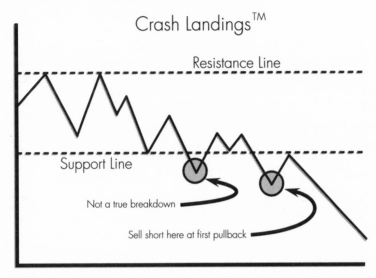

pull up a two-, three-, or four-hour chart. If you are a swing trader, you might want to track prices on a daily and weekly basis. The time horizon you measure is a mouse click away and the software will automatically adjust the bands to the time horizon measured. You set them to match your specific trading strategy (see Figure 4-2). The range that a stock will trade in between these support and resistance levels is known as the *accumulation range*. The process of a stock bouncing off of support and climbing to a point of resistance and then falling is called *channeling*.

The ability to recognize this pattern recognition is a very simple technique that can yield tremendous results. This technique will draw heavily on the need to monitor a Level II screen and watch the market makers positioning themselves as buyers when the stock nears a support level, and as sellers when a stock nears resistance.

It is important not to be too literal when using this approach as the section in this chapter on Sonic Booms and Crash Landings will explain. If the market makers seem to change their spots, so to speak, when you suspect them to react as they have in the past, you

FIGURE 4-5 *Some traders use the channels they create as entry and exit signals when trading "well behaved" stocks.*

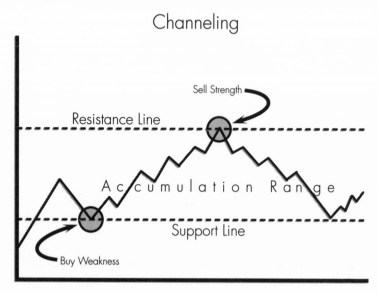

Channeling

may be heading for a breakdown or breakout. If this is the case and it is not recognized, losses can occur quickly. For example, if you suspect a stock is at support because of the pattern, but the market makers that influence the stock the most in the time horizon you are measuring are not returning to buy and accumulate, this stock may be heading for a breakdown. If you open a long position at the support level, and a breakdown occurs, you need to fire a market order and exit the trade immediately to cut losses.

This technique is a tremendous profit generator, but if using the charts is your only strategy for decision making and not following the more important indicators shown on the Level II screen, you will have some tough lessons ahead of you! Use the Level II screen to make decisions; use charts to reinforce them.

The highest highs and highest lows define the resistance points. The lowest highs and lowest lows signify support. The price movement between these levels is known as the accumulation range. The trader buys weakness (support) and sells strength (resistance) before the stock actually bounces off these imaginary lines. Keep in mind, buying at the bottoms and selling at the tops is extremely difficult and not very realistic. A good trader realizes this and buys stock on the way down and sells on the way up, while the majority of the market is on the other side. For example, if you are buying Applied Materials (AMAT) at 35, you want to buy as it weakens and the stock nears support while other traders are selling the weakness. And vice versa, when you are selling while the stock is still approaching resistance levels, as shown in Figure 4-2.

It is important to think of these lines as flexible and moveable rubber. Trading in the range within the time horizon you define is the goal. Your speculation in the trade is within the accumulation range. And you should avoid trying to hit the very bottom of the support and very top of the resistance. Unless you have a crystal ball or money to burn, don't be greedy or think you're that good, most aren't.

Keep market liquidity in the back of your mind. If the stock price is approaching the resistance line, all the other market participants will recognize the stock is in an "overbought" area. They will also begin to sell, and you will not be able to exit the trade at the resistance points, because millions of shares are headed for the exit gate, which is only large enough for thousands of shares. That puts you behind the trade instead of ahead of it—this is critical. If the market is a "net sellers" market, who will be willing to buy? Liquidity is the key, if you want to sell, someone must be willing to buy. As John D. Rockefeller once said, "I have made more money in the stock market selling too soon." So sell your long positions or open your shorts while the rest of the market perceives the stock as still strong. They will be buying, providing the liquidity you need to sell whenever you want. This can not be emphasized enough. The novice trader who does not learn this lesson pays dearly for not paying attention.

Sonic Booms (in Figure 4-3) are breakouts through a resistance line. I call them that because, like a jet, once the breakthrough takes place, you are headed for a wild ride. When a stock breaks through resistance, E-DAT traders want to own that stock. You must also limit your risk of buying immediately because a resistance level is not made of glass. It is more flexible and often gives the trader the illusion that it has broken, when in fact it has not, and the stock tends to retrace back toward support within the accumulation range. Therefore, to limit risk substantially, look for another technical indicator to help you detect if resistance has in fact really been broken. This analytic tool is the "first pullback" reaction following a real breakout. Remember, these tools are not literal interpretations but "decision support tools" that aid you in trading decisions.

The first pullback occurs when a stock seems to have broken resistance and then retraces back or pulls back and starts to reverse. At the pullback's low, the stock again reverses upward and the low of the pullback is at, above, or slightly below resistance. The buy signal comes when the pullback, after nearing the resistance line, moves above resistance a second time with strong volume. Here is where you buy and let the afterburners kick in. In theory, this stock is ready to soar. It has broken the resistance level and has broken the perception that it could not go higher than the resistance level, which is by definition what the resistance level is.

Once that perception is breached, the stock should take off. Listen for a Sonic Boom! Market orders are suggested here, or set a buy stop limit at the price near the first pullback after the breakout.

Always remember not to be too literal. You need to watch for reaction and how the stock is responding. When you start to see weakness in volume, you need to cover the trade immediately.

Crash Landings are the same as Sonic Booms but to the downside. They are breakdowns. When the stock price breaks a support level, it goes lower than the trading community thought that it would. Once this occurs, the stock, in theory, plunges at an accelerated rate.

Risk management principles should be applied. Once the stock breaks support, the trader opens a short position after the first pullback. Once again, in order to recognize the true breakdown, look for the first pullback. If the stock price does not reach the support line after the pullback, this indicates a true breakdown.

It is important to mention that in order to get short, you must sell into the buying market which creates the pullback, in order to get an uptick. This will almost always require more risk elasticity, since you should expect the stock to continue to rise a bit once the short is opened. Your tolerance for risk will need to be a bit greater with breakdowns, allowing more "heat" until the stock reverses and falls below your short entry price. It is important not to allow too much heat, but enough to give the trade a chance. I will typically not employ this strategy for momentum trading. As mentioned above, these are more typical of a one- to three-day swing trade.

VOLUME

Volume is a representation of liquidity, without which trading could not take place. Volume is the fuel that makes stock move. Without it nobody gets off the ground. If a stock is actively being purchased, it will rise. If it is sold more than it is being purchased, it falls. The degree that this takes place is measured by volume. The more transactions taking place, the faster the stock moves. This is why you must monitor volume. It is the spark that ignites a stock into motion. Once you see the volume, such as massive buying or selling by the professional trading community, you can chart the upward or downward move to determine when to open a position.

HEAVY AND LIGHT

Technical analysts often look for a larger point move in a stock over a longer time horizon. The information on Sonic Booms, Crash Landings, and what is to follow will help you see patterns to help you enter and exit trades for one- to five-day periods. As you think about why you might want to hang in on a trade for a longer time frame to realize a bigger point move, you must also think about how to limit risk.

In the momentum trades described earlier, you limited your risk with time. You only exposed yourself to market risk for a short time frame, but you traded "heavy." Heavy refers to trading in high share volume for a limited time, settling for a smaller, incremental move.

This is a risk-management tool but also accentuates the profitability of the trade. If you make only an ⅛ point on the trade and trade 1000 shares (heavy), the effect is plus or minus $125 (1000 × ⅛ or $0.125 = $125.00). Conversely, trading 500 shares (light) for a larger move of ¼ point, equates to the same profit or loss. Limit risk with time to offset the added risk of trading in high volume or vice versa. If you stay in a trade for longer periods of time, trade "light" with smaller share volume.

Understanding when volume kicks in, and what the directional bias of the stock is, will be the most important information to take from this chapter. Think of volume as the consensus or what the professional money believes as a whole. When the professional trading community sees something about to happen, they rush in to take a stake. It is not unlike a gold rush where speculators of old were not much different from speculators today, meaning they will step on each other to get to the mother lode. Volume is the indication of how much and fast they will rush in. Here are some technical indicators or signals to understand regarding volume and the effect it has on breakouts, breakdowns, consolidations, stabilization patterns, and directional bias:

- Thermal pressure occurs when there is big volume in a stock, which should move the stock price but does not. This tends to indicate that a reversal in the stock is about to take place, once the volume begins to subside. This works on both sides of the market. The reversal could be on the upside or the downside (see Figure 4-6).
- Big volume during a breakout or breakdown advances the move in either direction faster for more severe moves, which will also tend to be short lived. Like a jet in a severe climb, it will not hold that angle of attack very long without leveling off for a breather. Whether you see a Sonic Boom or Crash Landing, when the volume is very large, the moves tend to be accelerated and larger, but shorter lived.
- Low volume tends to spell consolidation or stabilization, or a lack of movement in price or directional bias. As low activ-

FIGURE 4-6   *Thermal pressure holds stocks up, until volume subsides. Then you can expect Crash Landings.*

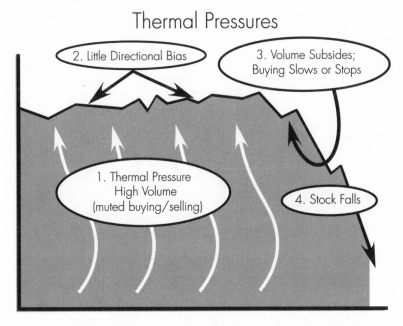

ity in the stock continues, the price of the stock tends to stay relatively stable or consolidated. Consolidation is a building up of pressure that generally leads to a move to the upside, once the volume begins to build again. Stabilization is an event that suggests the stock is about to show additional weakness, once the volume returns and is considered "bearish" for a stock. When the volume returns after a period of stabilization and the stock falls to a support level, the stock will tend to resist falling any further. See Figure 4-7. Once the volume diminishes again, the opposite of thermal pressure takes place and you see what I call the "suction effect."

• The suction effect occurs when there is downward pressure on the stock, which is defined by high volume and downward directional bias. When the stock resists falling any more, even though there is substantial downward pressure, the stock will rise rapidly once this downward pressure is

FIGURE 4-7   *When you see the combination of low volume and sideways price movement, this is not the chart of a stock to trade, especially for the short-term.*

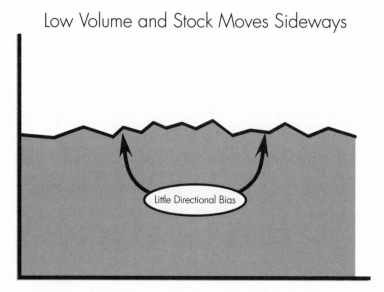

Low Volume and Stock Moves Sideways

Little Directional Bias

released or the volume subsides, which in effect "sucks" the stock back up to a resistance level. See Figure 4-8. This is the direct opposite of the thermal effect.

- Angle of attack measures how severe the move is. A severe move spells a short-lived event. A less dramatic move (either direction) indicates a more sustainable pattern. See Figures 4-9, 4-10, and 4-11.

OTHER TECHNICAL INDICATORS TO WATCH

Remember that these technical indicators do not signal absolutes. They are valuable tools to help you find stocks to trade, know when to enter a trade, when to exit, and how to trade the opening and the close (the best time to trade), anticipate moves, and use past events to forecast future ones (trend extension). Now let's focus on:

FIGURE 4-8 *The suction effect pulls stock prices to support levels. Eventually volume overcomes the pressure and prices move higher.*

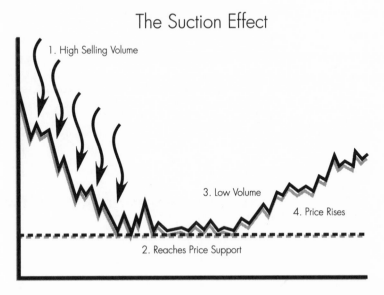

The Suction Effect

1. High Selling Volume

3. Low Volume

4. Price Rises

2. Reaches Price Support

FIGURE 4-9 *The angle at which the price of a stock goes up or down determines the length and distance of the move. The steeper the angle of attack, the shorter the duration of the move.*

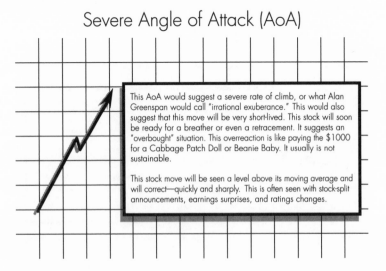

Severe Angle of Attack (AoA)

This AoA would suggest a severe rate of climb, or what Alan Greenspan would call "irrational exuberance." This would also suggest that this move will be very short-lived. This stock will soon be ready for a breather or even a retracement. It suggests an "overbought" situation. This overreaction is like paying the $1000 for a Cabbage Patch Doll or Beanie Baby. It usually is not sustainable.

This stock move will be seen a level above its moving average and will correct—quickly and sharply. This is often seen with stock-split announcements, earnings surprises, and ratings changes.

FIGURE 4-10   *If the angle of attack is slightly above the moving average of the stock's price, the price movement will be of medium duration.*

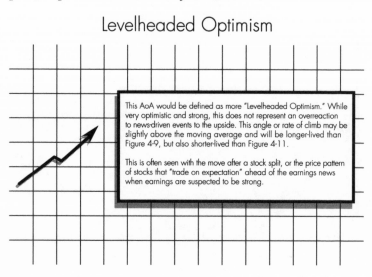

Levelheaded Optimism

This AoA would be defined as more "Levelheaded Optimism." While very optimistic and strong, this does not represent an overreaction to news-driven events to the upside. This angle or rate of climb may be slightly above the moving average and will be longer-lived than Figure 4-9, but also shorter-lived than Figure 4-11.

This is often seen with the move after a stock split, or the price pattern of stocks that "trade on expectation" ahead of the earnings news when earnings are suspected to be strong.

FIGURE 4-11   *A very modest angle of attack signifies a long, sustained price move. Think of the angles of attack as runners. A sprinter runs very fast for a short period of time. A miler goes farther, but slower. A marathon runner goes the longest distance, but also over the longest period of time.*

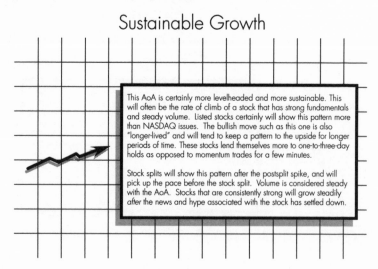

Sustainable Growth

This AoA is certainly more levelheaded and more sustainable. This will often be the rate of climb of a stock that has strong fundamentals and steady volume. Listed stocks certainly will show this pattern more than NASDAQ issues. The bullish move such as this one is also "longer-lived" and will tend to keep a pattern to the upside for longer periods of time. These stocks lend themselves more to one-to-three-day holds as opposed to momentum trades for a few minutes.

Stock splits will show this pattern after the postsplit spike, and will pick up the pace before the stock split. Volume is considered steady with the AoA. Stocks that are consistently strong will grow steadily *after* the news and hype associated with the stock has settled down.

- Shining Stars™
- The Emotional Hedge™
- Gap openings
- Leading indicators
- Advancers and decliners

SHINING STARS

Shining Stars are simply stocks or indexes that stand out from the crowd. *Investors Business Daily* calls them Relative Strength Leaders. The market seems to move in cycles in terms of sectors where trading is active. At times financial and banks stocks are in heavy play due to mergers and acquisitions. Other times oil drillers are getting a lot of attention. The technology sectors seem to always have some action and the S&P 500 is the index of choice for many professionals, particularly mutual funds. Therefore why not look for the shining stars in these industries, sectors, and indexes?

For example, if the stocks of the S&P 500 are outperforming the DJIA in percentage or relative strength and the technology sector of the S&P 500 is leading the S&P 500, the stocks that are performing strongest within the tech sector are good stocks to add to your watch list. These stocks are shining above the rest. For example, if Yahoo, an Internet stock, is up 10 points on the day and you look at the Chicago Board of Options Exchange Internet Index and find that that index is up as well, you could compute the percentage the stock is up for the day by comparing it to what the index is up for the day. If the stock is up more than the index, this stock is shining brighter than the rest of the stocks within that index. It could be a stock worth adding to your hit list. This is not a new idea, but one that many traders overlook. Many traders seem to follow the news today and go where the chaos is. Good traders go to the stocks that are quietly performing well and out of the spotlight in terms of the news, but in the spotlight in terms of the group sector of its index.

If you like the news-driven events that have the potential to drive stock prices higher or lower, consider earnings events. They almost always cause a stir, especially if the announcement does not reflect the market's expectation. Stock splits are another market event that almost always gives the stock a boost. They are often stocks that are experiencing strong earnings, trading in a high range by comparison with their 52-week high, etc. Or search for stocks with low price-earnings ratios. These are good finds—as are stocks heavily traded by mutual funds, because the size of mutual fund trades can be market movers by themselves. You can find these stocks by reviewing prospectuses of the best growth mutual funds.

As a trader, it is important to continually do the research to find attractive stocks to trade. Many Web sites will show earnings, stock splits, research, etc., to make your task easier for you, but you must decide what the criteria will be. I personally like the technology sector because it fascinates me and I enjoy reading about it. This way research isn't boring. I read for enjoyment while gaining valuable research for trading.

THE EMOTIONAL HEDGE

The Emotional Hedge is what I refer to when a trader uses technical indicators to enter, maintain, and exit trades automatically. Many new traders lack the discipline to cut losses quickly and need fences to run into that "force" them to exit a trade. Technical analysis offers many of these fences. The reason that discipline is needed by new traders is explained by the old truism, "There are old pilots and there are bold pilots, but there are very few old, bold pilots." The same is true for traders, few survive without discipline. Therefore, this section teaches you some methods of using technical indicators to help you exit trades successfully. Two great books I recommend when teaching risk management are *The Art of War,* by Sun Tzu, and *Reminiscences of a Stock Operator,* by Edwin Lefevre.

A third book that I recommend has nothing to do with trading but a great deal to do with attitude and taking responsibility, which does relate heavily to trading: *Learned Optimism,* by Dr. Martin Seligman. A trader's attitude about dealing with losses is one of the most important attributes a trader can have. One concept that I'll mention from Seligman's book, which I feel is particularly important for E-DAT traders, is that winners always recognize when they are wrong and act accordingly. Losers rationalize and forget what they were really trying to accomplish. Traders who have trades going against them rationalize by saying to themselves "It has to come back" or "It's a good company with good fundamentals, I can't go wrong with IBM!" They rationalize why they are holding a stock longer than they would have if it had been a profitable trade.

Seligman also says winners see positive events that happen to them as permanent. Negative things are seen as temporary. Negative people see positive events as lucky and temporary, and they see negative events as permanent. E-DAT traders must train themselves to maintain the most positive outlook possible. If you feel you cannot, it is a sign that E-DAT trading may not be for you.

Technical indicators are electric fences. If you brush against one of them, you get a shock. They are there to enforce trading discipline. Their purpose is to remind you to exit trades in a timely fashion—always cut your losses short. That is one of the most important tenets of E-DAT trading. Since technical signals are logical and unemotional, they are easy and automatic to follow. That is your Emotional Hedge!

A good trader can make money being right only 30 to 40 percent of the time. Think of your trading track record as a baseball batting average. If you had a lifetime batting average of over 300, you would be headed to the Baseball Hall of Fame. Concentrate on hitting singles (¼-point winners) and doubles (½-pointers) and the home runs will come naturally. You let your profits run when you are on the right side of the trade and cut trades immediately when you loose the perspective of the trade. By the way, you can be out-of-the-money in a trade a bit and still be successful by staying in it, but you must know where the risk elasticity is, when it is breached, and then you are out. This style of trading loses very little when wrong, and it avoids getting thrown into 10-foot ditches. Instead, it only trips over an occasional pothole.

Other traders are right 80 percent of the time or even more—and still lose money. They lose more by holding losing trades than they make on their winners. In *Reminiscences of a Stock Operator,* the lead character, Livingston, has this problem as a young 20-year-old trader. Learn from his mistakes, it is cheaper than learning from your own.

Beginning traders should use technical analysis for trade maintenance. Set mental stops and technical stops. Follow them rigorously to keep profits and minimize loses.

GAP TRADING

Stocks often trade very differently going into the close. The reason can be explained in an old industry axiom, "Amateurs control the open, professionals control the close." Most traders open positions in the morning. This is especially true of the average investor and, by far, the majority of them trade the opening from the long side. As an E-DAT trader you should be aware of another special circumstance that feeds into the gaps that are often seen on the opening, the "short squeeze," and the "hook close."

When professionals actively buy a stock going into the close after a down day, it is often the short squeeze at work. The buying by the professionals will rally a stock going into the close and create what would look like a "hook" on a chart. Understanding what is happening will help you avoid falling victim to this close and also give you several opportunities to profit from it.

This play is often seen on down days, when there are a lot of short sellers in the market. As the individual traders who are short see the close begin to rally as a result of the professionals buying stock, they often panic and are forced to cover their shorts. The professionals stand ready to sell into the buying short covers and are getting short themselves. First, they create the panic by buying, then get short themselves as the public or amateurs panic and cover their shorts. At this point, the buyers who are covering their shorts pick it up where the professionals left off and this is where the strong "hook" close occurs.

This will often continue the next day and the stock will gap open, instilling even more panic in the minds of amateur short sellers who held on overnight. The professionals will continue to sell to the amateurs who are buying to cover. Now the professionals are selling at inflated prices due to the strong hook close followed by a gap opening. Once the volume of buying subsides indicating most of the amateur shorts are covered, the stock falls very quickly after the open to allow the professionals to cover their shorts for a nice profit. This keeps the amateurs guessing and always one step behind.

Remember that many professional traders opened shorts at the close. If the market does not provide enough sellers for the buyers who wish to purchase and cover their shorts, the market makers sell short to fill the demand. Market makers are like car dealers, they want to sell stock as a rule, not buy it.

E-DAT traders can play it a few ways. Understanding this professional trading technique and recognizing it allows you to play a number of different ways, which I bet you can already envision. First, you could buy stocks that close strong. But you must understand that these longs should be covered very quickly the next day, since the professionals will be looking to cover their shorts opened at the close and the early morning. The E-DAT trader can also take the longer-term trade by opening a short at the close, like the professionals, and wait for the reversal of the gap opening. Either way, the E-DAT trader can recognize this squeeze, generally occurring on a down day, decide which side to take, and hold the stock for the appropriate time horizon and strategy. Although this seems a bit complicated, it is what traders need to recognize if they are going to trade gap openings, either to the upside or downside.

LEADING INDICATORS

The S&P 500 futures and long bond (30-year bond) are perhaps the finest short-term trading indicators you can follow.

Reading the tape is also a skill the successful trader needs to learn. The systems and tools available today are well worth the investment to be able to see live markets in real time on Level II. An average system costs a few hundred dollars a month, but this cost will be made up by as little as one trade if used properly. The tape and a Level II can allow you to see the stock and where it is heading before it hits the charts. Here are a few indications to look for on this leading indicator:

- If a stock is starting to show a reversal, the tape will indicate the stock failing to meet new highs. When this is observed it should be perceived as a precursor to a reversal or at least a downtrend. This will be seen on the Time and Sales screen.
- The correlation between the trades or "prints" on the Time and Sales screen and the movement of the market makers is also a huge tool. If the trades you see on the tape are trading at the offer price and the market makers are leaving the offer side of the Level II at that same offer price, the indication is bullish. This is especially true if the stock is near new highs for the day and has not run through any price levels. This would signal the beginning of an uptrend. The reverse is also true for downtrends. If the market makers are being hit by SOES traders and are leaving the bid, it signals a bearish situation.

ADVANCERS AND DECLINERS TABLES

The advancers and decliners numbers show you which stocks and stock sectors are showing strength and the performance of market leaders within indices. For example, the advance-decline numbers can be found on real-time systems, Web sites, and newspapers, which will tell you if more stocks are up than down. Take a look at the NYSE for a one-week period (see Figure 4-12).

Technical analysts use the average net advancers/decliners as a gauge of market direction and sentiment in addition to the DJIA. A technical analyst watches to see which stocks have moved most significantly within a given sector. For example, knowing that on Monday the majority of advancers are financial stocks while many

FIGURE 4-12 *The advance/decline table is one of the handiest and most reliable technical analysis tools. It shows you which stocks and stock sectors are showing the most strength. This is your clue to where to look for winners.*

Advancers/Decliners Table					
	Mon.	Tues.	Weds.	Thurs.	Fri.
Advancers	1600	1850	2100	2250	1500
Decliners	1500	1300	1700	1300	2450
Net advancers/decliners	100	550	400	950	−950
Weekly average	100	325	350	500	210

decliners are in the technology sector, would help you focus on the hot area—depending on your inclination to trade long or short.

Additionally, when the overall market begins to peak, the average starts to erode. Keep in mind that the broader the base of the measurement is over time, the less volatile the average is. You can plot this information to measure market strength over any time frame. When a period of selling occurs, the average is negative. But when it begins to gain some strength, it shows you the market or a stock is approaching a support level and is beginning to come back.

What I like about this technical indicator is that you can measure whatever you desire with the simple calculations as shown above. This is perhaps the best barometer to measure a sector or group of stocks from a broader perspective. If you are trading DELL and the advancers/decliners for computer manufacturers are net down for three consecutive days, you might think twice before opening a long position for anything but a momentum trade.

As you can see, technical analysis can be very simple or complicated. Many traders have mistaken activity for accomplishment by staying very busy doing calculations, studying charts, reading the stars, etc., but they never seem to accomplish anything, that is, make trades. Remember, trading is a journey not a destination. If you wait to get all the knowledge you think you need, you will never leave ground school!

CHAPTER 5

THINKING LIKE AND TRADING WITH THE NASDAQ MARKET MAKERS

Think of the NASDAQ market makers as the air traffic controllers of the over-the-counter markets. Because they are so important to successful electronic direct access trading, you need more information about them.

Just as air traffic controllers spend their working days hunched over radarscopes, the NASDAQ market makers resist leaving their Level II trading screens while the stock market is open. As mentioned before, NASDAQ is a screen-based market. Each stock traded has at least two market makers. No single market maker knows every bid and ask or how high the stack of orders is behind each bid and ask as a whole the way a specialist would on a listed stock. All this uncertainty can be used to your advantage. That's why it is so critical to successful E-DAT trading to spend some time learning the tendencies of market makers and shadowing them as E-DAT traders.

NASDAQ was created on February 5, 1971. At the moment, it is the third largest stock market and fastest-growing in the world, especially when you take into account its proposed merger with the American Exchange in New York and potential mergers with other regional exchanges. Technology is king on the NASDAQ and the business marketplace, therefore, NASDAQ is well positioned for more substantial growth.

The only negative in the system was the way retail orders use to be handled. The market makers kept the spread between the bid and ask wide. Oddly enough, this had become an unbelievable positive for you. This problem lead to new order-handling rules and provided direct access to the market makers by you, an individual retail customer. This chapter explains just how you can take advantage of all these changes.

Battles have been fought on the issues surrounding the way business is done on the NASDAQ, and the changes that have resulted definitely have benefited the American public. But none of that matters if a electronic trader can not recognize what is going on in the markets or a stock. Many firms, and you see them on television, boast of their "superior" systems to trade on and their low commissions of $7.95, which we now know is smoke and mirrors due to "paid for order flow." Additionally, without market insight and intuitive skills to recognize what is happening at a given moment, those tools and low commissions are simply the vehicles of pain for the new, unsuspecting, bright-eyed trader.

The next section will bridge the gap from where you are now and deliver you to the most advanced trading platforms available married to the skill needed to read this information. I once asked an attendee at one of my seminars what he would do with real-time market data if it were in front of him and, as I suspected, the person had no idea. As you move into the Level II section, think about the psychology and motivation of why market makers position themselves the way they do on this system and you will begin to separate the fact from the fiction and reveal their true trading patterns.

NASDAQ LEVEL II TRADING SCREEN

There is no more powerful trading tool available to the short-term trader than the NASDAQ Level II screen. Most brokers today still don't have one. Level II provides you with the current quotes and the sizes of the quotes available from each market maker in a security. The data shown on a Level II can be configured to show alert traders a number of trends in a security and the most prominent market maker in that security. If you can learn to read the Level II screen, you can be a successful E-DAT trader. First, let's look at the basic functions of Level II.

Advancements in trading software have substantially enhanced the usefulness of the Level II screen. Software programs, such as my TradeWise™ system powered by Real Tick III, The Attain system, CyberTrader, and Speer Leeds & Kellogg RediSystem provide traders with analysis and insights into market activity. For example, instead of just showing you how many times a market maker like Goldman Sachs is the bidder, the new breed of software also nets out the total of all market makers to give you an indication of a net buyers or net sellers market. This net buying or selling indication provides a much clearer picture of what is happening. These calculations, based on the Level II information, now interpret the directional bias of the stock. Simply put, systems today do much of the math for you so you can focus on interpreting the information and trading. Think of a Level II screen in a live market as a radar screen; you get to see virtually every player in the stock in real time, and your ability to read their pattern will tell you if the stock is gaining, losing, or maintaining altitude.

Many new E-DAT traders feel they need every analytical tool on the planet in order to make a decision to open a trade, but give me a Level II, time and sales screen and an execution system and I can trade. More isn't necessarily better when trading. If you can get your head into what is going on from Level II, you have 95 percent of what it takes to enter, maintain, and exit positions!

THE INSIDE MARKET

The Level II screen is divided into two halves; on the left side are the market makers and their bids. These are arranged in descending order, the best (highest) bid, known as the *high bid,* being at the top.

On the right side are the market makers and their offers (ask). These are arranged in ascending order, the best (lowest) offer, or low offer, at the top. See Figure 5-1.

Each of the bids and offers displayed on the system is shown with the size (number of shares) that the market maker must honor at that price. The best bid and best offer is referred to as the *inside market*. This is usually the price at which traditional retail clients are quoted and the price they get. It is not always the best price that can be accessed by a trader, using SelectNet, InstiNet, and the other ECNs. As you will learn, you are often able to sell on the offer (ask) and buy on the bid, thus saving money on the spread. This is something that only market makers used to be able to do.

Let's look at an example. If you owned 1000 shares of QCOM Computer and wanted to sell it, you would naturally want the best

FIGURE 5-1 *The Level II market maker screen is the serious trader's crystal ball. It lets you see what strategies the market makers are attempting. Once you know that, you can shadow the professionals and trade like an insider.*

Level II Market Maker Screen

Name	Bid	Size	#Best	Name	Bid	Size	#Best
MSCO	64 1/2	10	10	LEHM	64 9/16	10	13
HRZG	64 3/8	10	3	INCA	64 9/16	10	72
GSCO	64 3/8	10	7	PRUS	64 5/8	10	10
MLCO	64 3/8	5	6	CHGO	64 5/8	10	3
JPMS	64 3/8	10	4	NITE	64 5/8	5	6
PWJC	64 1/4	10	2	DEAN	64 5/8	2	5
NFSC	64 1/4	10	5	COWN	64 5/8	10	2
SHWD	64 1/4	10	1	ISLD	64 5/8	5	119
OLDE	64 1/4	10	3	MONT	64 3/4	10	8
SBSH	64 1/4	10	7	SNDV	64 3/4	10	2
DEAN	64 1/4	10	0	SBSH	64 3/4	10	9
RSSF	64 1/8	10	8	MASH	64 3/4	10	20
TSCO	64 1/8	10	3	MLCO	64 3/4	10	6
SNDV	64 1/8	10	0	BEST	64 3/4	10	6
MADF	64 1/8	5	0	NFSC	64 13/16	1	3
PERT	64 1/8	10	3	DMGL	64 7/8	10	1
LEHM	64 1/8	10	23	HRZG	64 7/8	10	6
HMQT	64 1/16	10	1	RSSF	64 7/8	10	0
DMGL	64	10	3	PERT	64 7/8	10	7
MONT	64	10	8	ABSB	64 7/8	3	3
				HMQT	65	10	8

possible price. The highest buyer in the market for QCOM stock at that exact moment would be the inside bid, or high bid. If you wanted to own QCOM stock, you would want to pay as little as possible. Therefore, you would seek out the lowest seller of QCOM, which would be the inside offer, or low offer. The power to see where the market makers stand in terms of their willingness to buy or sell is all represented on the Level II screen.

The power of the Level II is that market makers have no place to hide. If they are buyers of the stock, you see it by their bids. If they are sellers, you see their low offers. The ability to see the market in session tells the tale of where the stock is going. Being able to see the bids and asks change in real time is called *transparency*. You, the average trader, see what every professional sees. Experience in reading this movement is paramount to your success. The Level II radarscope allows you to see all the market participants and where they are headed, but you do not always know their final destination. The more experience you develop in tracking the market makers, the more accurate your judgment becomes as to their intentions. This leads you to strategies to shadow and front-run their moves. Both of these approaches provide you with winning trades.

THE OUTSIDE MARKET

Any market maker's bid or offer, that is not the inside market, is considered "away" from the market or "out-of-the-money." The firms or market makers that are bidding low or offering high do not attract anyone. Why would I sell to Montgomery Securities (MONT) if that firm is bidding less than Morgan Stanley (MSCO)? Montgomery at the bottom of the bid list will attract no sellers (see Figure 5-1). Since these prices are not the inside market, why do we care?

When you are evaluating a trade—and whether or not to enter into or close out that trade—it is important to know the momentum of the stock. By looking at the crowd of market makers beneath the inside bid (lower prices) or beneath the low offer (higher prices), you are able to gauge the strength of the current inside market. If there is more than one market maker on the inside bid, you can make a determination of the strength of that bid. If there is only one market maker at that bid, you can see what bid is below the inside level and how many market makers are at the next levels. By viewing this on the Level II screen, you get a micro visual impression of the forces of supply and demand at work—about as pure a form of capitalism as you'll find anywhere.

Looking at the outside market is like studying the foundation of a home. If you see cracks and other signs of deterioration, you know that sooner or later the structure must collapse. If you see it is strong, upward bias may be about to occur. If the outside market's bids are breaking down—even before weakness appears in the inside market—you have an insight as to what could happen to the inside market. The weakness is first seen when the number of market makers bidding decreases. The demand is breaking down, a sure sign that price will follow suit. Or if the crowd doing the bidding begins to grow and become more aggressive, prices are about to head north.

On the opposite side, if the number of offers increases and the current offer price is replaced by a lower offer price, you know there is stock for sale and supply is surpassing demand. This, of course, means price deterioration. Or if offer activity and prices pick up, you know prices are going north. As anyone from Los Angeles can tell you, when the foundation begins to move, the rest of the house isn't far behind. Savvy traders look for clues as to what the inside market is going to do by paying close attention to the bids and offers of the outside market. It is usually the market on the level right below the inside market that is the messenger of what is to come.

Let's talk about supply and demand for a moment because that is what Level II represents. Capitalism is the greatest achievement of the Western world in terms of economics—a true checks and balances system that as a whole self-corrects when the forces of supply and demand fall out of equilibrium. Other economies that have competed with this concept seem to have failed on a global scale. The Level II is simply a representation of supply and demand in the most actively traded market in the world, the stock market!

When supply exceeds demand, prices fall, when demand exceeds supply, prices rise. When supply continues to grow in excess of demand, prices will plummet, and when demand far exceeds supply, prices will find inflationary levels that will jettison upward. While reading a Level II system, you are simply seeing the forces of supply and demand at work in a given stock. The market makers are the merchants of the marketplace, and their willingness to buy and sell will be represented by their quotations. If one market maker bids the highest for the stock and others soon follow, the stock is likely to climb; if suddenly a market maker lowers the price of stock for sale and others follow, the price is heading south. The system is self-policing because if at any time there is no more supply at a given price, the market will bid more for the stock to attract sellers happy to sell at a higher level. If no seller comes forward, which will be represented by no supply of stock for sale at this new sale price, the stock will move to a higher price and continue until someone comes forward to sell, in order to meet demand. **Pure capitalism!** What better system is there than that? It is hard to believe this level of information has been kept from the American public for so long. How it could have been forbidden to window shop for stock with this efficient system for so long still baffles me, but it is here now and the only barrier to your success will be your skill in shopping, aka trading.

You see this stuff is really quite simple in concept, and if you keep the broader perspective, you will always see the forest for the trees and not get lost in the wilderness, the way the professionals hope that you will. Our traditional, trusting wilderness guides, known as *brokers,* have lead us off the trail too many times and have breached our trust to the point that the power is now in your hands. In fact I may have just answered my own question of why this information was not available to us until recently. On a national scale, and I mean national, we would not put up with it anymore and we have as we have always done forced the wheels of change to turn, and pushed new rules through that have leveled the playing field.

In the defense of the brokers, I don't think they have been the force that has breached our trust, but more the tools of the firms that have breached our trust, the market makers. These firms have enjoyed artificially wide margins for too long, and the brokers were only the foot soldiers. In the end, fairness prevailed as it usually does in America and the markets are open for business for all to participate.

Think of the movement of the bid and ask on the Level II screen as the movements of the hands of an analog watch. When stock moves on the Level II screen from the offer to the bid (counterclockwise), the move is bullish. When the stock prices move from the bid to the offer (clockwise), the movement in price is bearish. This is a very key concept.

Clockwise motion = Bearish (weak)

If the bid prices begin to change to the offer prices, what the market maker paid for the stock (the bid) is now being offered for sale. If the market maker MSCO (Morgan Stanley) buys QCOM (QUALCOMM Inc.) at 64½ and moments later offers it for sale at the low offer price of 64⁹⁄₁₆ (¹⁄₁₆ spread), this is slightly bearish (Figure 5-1).

If as a result other market makers join that low offer price because they want to compete with MSCO as a seller, the supply of stock for sale at 64⁹⁄₁₆ would build. As supply increases, price and demand diminish, and prices will fall. Once enough sellers or market makers join the low offer price of 64⁹⁄₁₆, and supply at this price builds to a point where one of the sellers says, "Hey! It's too crowded in here for me. I'm going lower in price to be alone and become more attractive to buyers in the market by offering to sell cheaper." What would be that next low price, if you maintained a ¹⁄₁₆ spread? It would be the 64½, the former bid. The bid price moves from the bid to the offer and the screen scrolls clockwise or from left to right. That is a bearish move. See Figure 5-2.

Counterclockwise motion = Bullishness (strong)

Conversely, if suddenly the market makers begin a buying frenzy for QCOM and other market makers join MSCO as a bidder at

FIGURE 5-2 *The Time and Sale screen tells you the time, size and price of all trades as they take place. You know in real time where a stock is headed.*

Time and Sale Screen

Time & Sales

64 1 /2	1000
64 1 /2	1000
64 1 /2	1000
64 9/16	500
64 1 /2	1000
64 9/16	300
64 9/16	200
64 9/16	1000
64 9/16	500
64 9/16	600
64 9/16	1000
64 9/16	1000
64 19/32	1000
64 9/16	1000
64 9/16	1000

64½, the demand builds. If demand increases, supply generally diminishes and prices rise. MSCO is now in line with eight other bidders and says, "Hey guys, I was here first with the only bid on QCOM at 64½. I liked it that way. I'm leaving this price level and going back to being high bidder!" This would mean that MSCO revises its bid to a higher price, 64⁹⁄₁₆ (the former offer price) and stock begins to rise. The offer price moves from right to left or counterclockwise. That is a bullish move. See Figure 5-3.

Supply/demand = Pure capitalism

Level II is pure supply and demand at its finest. If the bids are building and the offers are fading, the stock movement is bullish. Or, if the bids are building, demand is building, and more market makers want to own the stock—the current price moves from outside the market to the inside bid price, or high bid. At the same time the supply is fading (or the offers are fading) because demand is taking hold of the market. All the buyers in the world that are watching the Level

FIGURE 5-3   *One of the easiest ways to stay tuned with the rhythm of the market is to keep an eye on the movement of the bid and ask. If the movement is counterclockwise, it is bullish. If clockwise, bearish.*

Bull and Bear Markets

Bullish Level II Screen

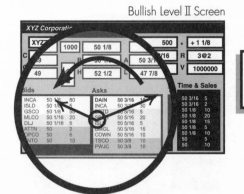

If the ASK prices become the BID prices, the stock is moving higher.

Bearish Level II Screen

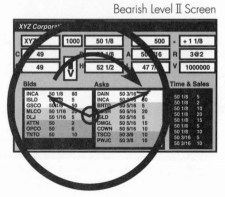

If the BID prices become the ASK prices, the stock is falling.

II suddenly think the offer price is not such a bad deal. They begin buying the stock at the offer price. The market makers, selling at this offer price, sell the stock to the buyers. Then they pull the offer, meaning they will not sell any more at that price because they now demand more for the stock.

In other words, a market maker who sells 1000 shares at 64⁹/₁₆, by joining the low offer price, may decide not to refresh his offer. This means that the market maker is not willing to sell any more stock at that price. Therefore, the offers fade because other market makers, selling at the low offer, are reacting the same way. As they sell the stock, they refuse to sell any more and pull themselves off the offer side of the market at that 64⅗ price. What may have been six market makers selling at this price now fades. They are filled because buyers force them to sell using SOES. Now there are only five, then four, three, etc., until there are no offers at that price.

When supply diminishes and demand builds, the stock is on the rise. This is pure supply and demand at work, but on a micro, one-stock, level. To me, it is beauty in motion.

TIME AND SALES

If the Level II screen is the lamp, the Time and Sales screen the bulb, they belong together and light the path to successful trading. Time and sales show actual trades and the time they went off, and at what size. As trades occur, market makers refresh or pull their quotes on the Level II. For example, if you placed Figures 5-1 and 5-2 together and watched the 64½ trades on the Time and Sales screen (Figure 5-2), it would appear that MSCO on the Level II bought 3000 shares, indicated by the last three sales called "prints" on the Time and Sales screen. If MSCO stays at the 64½ bid, that is a bullish indication evidenced by MSCO's appetite for QCOM (Buying). Soon, other market makers will want to compete with that bid and join MSCO. If that happens, it may set the stock in motion and the move would be counterclockwise by a higher bid of 64⅗ (right to left), or the former offer price becoming the new bid.

THE MARKET-MAKING BUSINESS

Now that you have a feel for the Level II screen, lets look closer at the market makers on the Level II screen and bring this all to life. During market hours the market makers bid and offer stock in order to make a two-sided market, they fill their customer orders and trade for their own accounts. Market markers are brokers and dealers, thus the term *broker-dealer*. The terms, market maker and broker-dealer, are somewhat synonymous, since all market makers must be broker-dealers, but not all broker-dealers are market makers. And, all broker-dealers must be members of the National Association of Security Dealers.

THE MARKET MAKER AS A BROKER

An understanding of the motivation of NASDAQ market makers, or broker-dealers, is important and explains why the NASDAQ has earned a reputation for price volatility compared to the NYSE. The NASDAQ has helped open the gates for individual traders, but the inherent characteristics of a negotiated market and the growth companies associated with the NASDAQ create volatility. You can trade both markets, but you must take two different approaches.

Here is a real example of the type of volatility I am talking about. Entremed, Inc. (ENMD), a drug manufacturing company, announced a potential cure for cancer on a Friday, after the market closed. The stock closed at $12. Upon the news, market makers began to bid this stock higher and higher on pure speculation of what they felt the stock was now worth. The stock was bid all the way up to $80 before one trade ever took place on Monday morning. Remember this is just representative of what market makers bid or said the stock was worth. If a company puts a man on Mars tomorrow, their stock would not move 700 percent in book value overnight, but this has been the case in many NASDAQ issues. The market makers bid this stock to this unrealistic level and the public caught wind of it very quickly. The result was a ton of market orders ready for the open on Monday morning. Dumb money, which is the uninformed investor, buys the stock at this "irrational, exuberant" price of $80 per share. Unfortunately, most of the public uses market orders, usually a mistake on an opening order, such as this example.

The professional community was more than happy to sell at this price from their inventory, or from the short side. A selling frenzy ensued. It was smart money selling overvalued stock to dumb money. Naturally, the public had their heads handed to them as the stock fell like a simonized safe in a matter of 45 minutes. Eventually it reached a level that was more realistic, approximately $40. In the meantime the investors who bought the stock at $80 were in a state of shock when they returned from their morning coffee break. My guess is that many took sick leave upon seeing the fall. By the way, when I refer to "dumb money," that is not meant to be derogatory or insulting, but is a term used by the professional trading community to describe the uninformed investors who enter the market and provide professionals liquidity to trade against.

My point: You must understand how market makers think and what motivates them to trade the way they do. Once you learn to read their radar, you can tune in, and use this information to your advantage. The market makers of the NASDAQ reach price consensus by negotiation. For this reason, they commonly bid stocks artificially high to protect themselves. Secondly, they are always trying to make a profit. For example, as the price goes higher and higher, they face the risk of being forced, by a customer, to prematurely sell stock out of inventory or borrow it from another broker-dealer and then have to pay that broker back, taking a loss. Bidding a stock artificially high allows the stock to find price equilibrium below their bids. Thus their downside is protected and they are in a position to sell their inventory of stock at a profit, or sell short and buy it back cheaper. If you learn to think like a market maker, you will not get whipsawed as the general public often does.

Another opportunity for E-DAT is to recognize market makers working large order for their customers. Always keep in mind that market makers, on the broker side of the trade, are paid commissions to fill orders for customers. Who are their biggest and best customers? The larger institutions, such as mutual and pension funds and money managers. These blue-chip accounts better get good fills or the brokers slip off the gravy train. The commission revenue can be as much as six cents per share, which can add up very quickly considering the volume involved. A trade of 100,000 shares is very normal to many of these firms.

Once you learn to spot these orders going down, you can pick up on the intention of the market makers and front-run on their trades. You cannot compete with these firms or match the volume they trade, but you can let them show you the trend when momentum trading. Or you can follow (shadow) these firms as part of a successful trading strategy. I call it "shadowing" because that is what you should do, move like them in their shadows.

These firms, while filling large orders, show you if they are net buyers or sellers. Following that direction is our goal. If they are buying, so should you. If they are selling, you sell. This information, which is on the Level II and Time and Sale screens, gives you a huge advantage by making you privy to the trading strategy of the major market makers.

When a market maker is advertising to buy or sell stock, it is expected to trade at least 200 shares at the quoted price. The seller of stock is always responsible for reporting the transaction. That way, you, the public, see what transactions take place. This report must be made within 90 seconds of completing the trade, but because the trade is done electronically, it is generally reported immediately.

If a market maker is bidding for stock, they can be filled up to 1000 shares at a time through the SOES system. If they want to buy more, they refresh the bid for another 1000 shares. If this continues, you recognize the market maker as a net buyer and will want to look closely for reaction to buys. You can trade so fast with ECNs that you can accomplish a buy and sell in seconds, catching an eighth- or a quarter-point profit. That's how you shadow a market maker.

When a dramatic move by a market maker is clear and obviously moving the stock or showing directional bias, the market maker is referred to as the *ax,* or the dominant influence in the stock at this particular moment. You follow the ax and harvest as many winners as you can. Here is an example of an ax in action.

A market maker has a large order to fill from Putnam. Instead of sitting on the bid, waiting to be SOESed, the market maker uses SelectNet or an ECN to acquire the stock needed to fill a large customer order. Here is how it happens.

Putnam: "I need 50,000 of Intel, what can you do?"

Market Maker: "I'll sell 30,000 at 90¼, 8,000 at 90⅜, 5,000 at 90½ and clean up the rest at 90⅝."

Putnam: "Do it," or "I'm in!"

In this example, the market maker has the order presold and needs to accumulate the stock at an average price lower than the sale promised to the institutional customer; that is how this market maker makes money. This market maker has an interest in driving prices lower to buy the stock or at least hide its buying appetite for these 50,000 shares. E-DAT traders like us can see the trade going down on our computer screens, evidenced by the strong buying posture this market maker is taking. Sure the market maker will do what it can to hide the order, by offering stock when it really wants to buy, but the E-DAT trader who can see this market maker at the bid, more than at the offer, recognizes it as a net buyer. Instead of being hit by the ax, you follow the ax, or shadow it, and trade like the lead market maker. You have the potential to make the same profit margin they make, with obviously a lower share volume.

If the buying firm knew another firm that had the stock to sell, it could send a message using the Preference Feature of SelectNet. That way the world would not know what it was doing and would not run the price of the stock higher. Because of the negotiated market, however, market makers do not know the order flow of other firms, as a specialist would for a listed stock, and therefore are forced to show their intentions by bidding for stock at the inside market.

Here are some additional indications that can be seen on the Level II screen:

- A market maker will not leave the bid after being SOESed for 1000 shares. This market maker just keeps taking 1000-share SOES orders from SOES and E-DAT traders. This means the firm has more orders to fill for this stock and it is showing you its hand by its unlimited buying appetite. It stays on the bid while other market makers and ECNs leave, this is bullish. (This behavior can also occur on the offer or ask side of the market, which would be bearish since continuous selling would depress stock prices.)

- The market maker "lifts an offer" or pays the retail price for the stock. Now the market maker is even willing to buy stock at the offer price. When you see this you need to move quickly without any hesitation and buy the stock. SOES the offer, so it is mandatory and the market maker fills you. Or if an ECN is the low offer, increase your limit order over the current low offer price to avoid chasing the stock.

If you understand the motivation and characteristics of the NASDAQ and market makers, you develop the radar necessary to be a successful E-DAT momentum trader. While many of these patterns that market makers show you seem simple, they require time in front of a live market watching and experiencing these moves. As you spend that time, you will gain the intuition needed to trade successfully. Only time and practice will give you this skill. Therefore, please feel free to contact our Web site as noted earlier to obtain a CD ROM where these patterns have been recorded. The confidence that you will gain when you know what is occurring before prices react will replace any fear you may have regarding trading with professionals on a Level II. They are just regular people with no clairvoyant power; you have access to the same tools they do.

The primary weapon systems of all the market makers are the same ones you will have access to as an E-DAT trader:

- SOES
- SelectNet
- ECNs

These systems were covered in Chapter 2, and once you harness their power along with the strategies in Chapters 7, 8, and 9 you will be ready to take control of your own financial destiny. Remember, retail broker-dealer firms do not send their brokers to Hawaii for how much money they make for you—it is for the money they bring into the firm. E-DAT allows you to take control of your own destiny.

THE MARKET MAKER AS A DEALER

When they are acting as dealers or making what are called *principal transactions,* market makers are trading for their own accounts. This means they are taking on transactions that incur market risk instead of filling riskless customer orders for a commission. Dealers are paid what is called a *markup,* which is generally limited to a maximum of 5 percent. Five percent is a guideline, not a hard-and-fast rule. Market makers are paid in one of these two ways, commissions as brokers or markups as dealers. The only reason they risk their capital in dealer transactions is to take profits, just as all traders do.

Security dealers are like any other dealership, only they buy and sell stocks. They make money when they can sell what they buy at a profit. Therefore, as a trader, you want to determine in which capacity the market makers are acting. Do they have their broker or their dealer hat on today? Why are they buying? Like car dealers, the only reason they buy your car (trade-in) is to sell you a new one. They want to buy your old car at a weak price so that they can sell it higher. Market makers do the same thing.

By the very nature of their name, market makers are willing to make a market in a stock. Most firms make markets in many different stocks, which gives them a vested interest in trading those stocks, especially if they were part of the original underwriting syndication.

The most riskless way a firm trades is by taking the spread. In 1996 the Justice Department concluded that these firms had colluded to keep spreads artificially wide. Because there were wide spreads, they could buy at the bid (wholesale) and sell at the offer (retail) and make a riskless profit on the spreads, when they should have been incurring the risks associated with being dealers in these transactions. Today, with tighter spreads, new rules, and speculation that the decimal system will be implemented by the twenty-first century, market makers need to trade more efficiently, just like us. Therefore, we are truly on an equal footing.

For example, buy INTC (Intel) at a 90 (bid) and sell it at 90¼ (offer). Simple enough, profitable enough. As a result of the Justice Department's investigation, spreads have come down dramatically in most liquid, highly traded, stocks like Intel. Now most liquid stocks trade with a spread of a *teenie,* or ¹⁄₁₆ of a point, and I suspect these spreads will continue to tighten.

As the twenty-first century approaches, I feel strongly that the system will go to decimal increments and further reduce spreads. This change will create an even more efficient market. In the old gold rush days, the miners rarely made money, but the smart money that sold the picks and shovels did just fine taking very little risk. Remember the car dealers, buying your used car as a trade-in cheap (weakness) and selling it to an excited new prospect looking for a new used car (strength). If you shadow the market makers, you reduce your risk as well, because they limit their risk by buying up others' fears and selling to others' irrational buying. Don't fall for the hype in the market; study what the "pros" are doing and follow.

LIFE EXPECTANCY OF TRADES

Broker (trades initiated for customers) transactions tend to be longer lived and larger in terms of point moves. In dealer, or principal transactions, they are for smaller incremental moves and tend to be short lived. The market makers, while executing orders for customers, are agents. The customers take all the risk. The money flowing into stocks to buy tends to stay there longer, because many of these customers are mutual funds, long-term investors, and other bulls who plan on buying and holding for a longer time frame and larger point move. Additionally, the institutions tend to buy in larger increments, which you can see by watching Level II and Time and Sale screens.

Conversely, when you study the Level II screen and determine that the trades are more consistent with dealer transactions, expect these moves to be short-lived and to be in small incremental price moves. The firms are now risking their own capital and they don't like market risk. They want to be in and out very quickly. What does that tell you about how you should trade?

When dealer-type trading is controlling a stock, the stock tends to trade in narrow ranges. The stocks swing back and forth very quickly (in 20-minute intervals). This is a perfect time to shadow market makers. Especially the market maker who is "the ax," or the most influential market maker in the stock at that time. In short, you act like a market maker—buy when they buy and sell when they sell. Your trades will be short-lived, fast movers, yielding small profits and utilizing larger numbers of shares (heavy). This is when momentum trading is at its best, a super opportunity for electronic day traders.

MARKET-MAKING

Recognizing in what capacity the market makers are trading allows you to trade with them. Remember, let the big firms make the markets and move them, that is their function as market makers. Your job is to find out how they are trading and tailgate. Here is one of their key plays.

Playing possum is a game in which a market maker appears to be showing weakness by going low offer consistently when in fact it is a buyer of the stock. The concept is simple. A market maker sells, for example 3000 shares, to show weakness in the stock. After the price falls, it buys back more than it sold at the new lower price, which makes this market maker a net buyer of stock, rather than a net seller. It buys more than it sells while the stock is falling, known as "averaging down. . . ." "Don't frown, average down!" is an old axiom that market makers say that describes how they instill panic in order to buy up the weakness. The way to spot this play is when you see a market maker move from high bid to low offer, but only stay on the offer for a short period of time compared to the time at the bid. It will move back and forth between the bid and offer. This strategy is easy to see. For example, BEST (Bear Sterns) bids AMAT (Applied Materials) at 35⅛, the current high-bid price. Moments later, it moves to the low offer of 35³⁄₁₆. Traders who watched them go low offer decide to sell and hit the bid to cover their trades.

As the various traders and investors (not the professionals) panic and begin to sell by hitting the 35⅛ bid with their SOES gun, BEST may return to take the hits! It buys up, let's say 10,000 shares at 35⅛. By not leaving the bid, BEST begins to show strength to the market by buying the stock at the 35⅛ bid. Other market makers may return, and ECNs, who want to compete and are at a lower bid price, may decide to join that 35⅛ bid price. BEST may leave the high bid and move lower to a bid of 35—while also offering stock it just bought at 35⅛. BEST just bought the stock at the bid of 35⅛ and is now offering it at 35⅛.

Why? Because it won't sell all 10,000 shares at this new low offer price, it will sell only enough to panic the traders who bought the previous offer at 35³⁄₁₆ or when the new bidders who joined the 35⅛ bid, prior to BEST moving to bid at 35. The result is more buying than selling to accumulate a position. As additional selling continues to depress the price, BEST continues to buy on the way down.

The first lesson to be learned when shadowing market makers is to determine who the "ax" is in the stock at a given moment. Then figure out what it is doing and join it—don't fight the "ax." When other market makers join the "ax," this is called *consensus*. Once you begin to see the stock change direction, take part of the profitable momentum trade. In this example, when BEST buys enough stock as it is falling, you should also buy when BEST completes its buying. The reason is, when BEST is finished buying, it will want to take profits at a higher price, and start to bid higher for the stock to show strength, which will help inflate prices, and cause many traders to jump in and buy. As this occurs, BEST will be selling more on the way up than it buys, which is exactly the opposite of what it did when accumulating the position, i.e., buying as it fell (buy weakness). BEST will sell into strength as the stock rises at average prices higher than it payed. This is the concept behind buy weakness, sell strength, and how market makers play possum.

ELECTRONIC DAY TRADING

It is helpful to understand the inherent differences between listed securities and the NASDAQ. "Whereas the intentions of traders in listed securities are usually masked and not easily obtainable, market makers on NASDAQ are constantly adding their names to markets as buyers or sellers of stocks. Profits will come easily to the day trader who can determine whether these specific market makers are simply fulfilling their responsibility to provide a two-sided market or are actual buyers or sellers of stock."* Furthermore, E-DAT with market makers allows the day trader to capitalize on intraday price fluctuations and momentum.

This opportunity is a bit different with listed securities. Listed securities offer other advantages. For example, when a stock begins to move on the NYSE, it tends to rally longer, which provides a good opportunity to get in and out with a profit without quite the speed required on NASDAQ.

There is certainly much to understand, but think of your head as a VCR with an empty shelf above it. As a new E-DAT, that is where you are. You have no video tapes to plug into your VCR (your brain). Accumulating trading ideas and strategies is equivalent to filling your shelf with tapes. Knowing when and what tape to play is the real science, so begin with a few theories you understand and like. After you start making trades with a certain strategy or technique, you will be amazed how fast you learn and how simple it can be. Once you feel secure, you will be adding more tapes exponentially, because ideas like these feed on each other, and that is when it starts to get really exciting.

In Chapter 6, I will discuss the process of defining who you are or want to be as a trader. This will depend very much upon your personality, time, and schedule, risk tolerance, and expectations. I have found that the most success with traders is when they trade within their means and personality. Defining what type of trading you will do is the first step to success. Anything less than formulating a spe-

---

*Friedfertig, Marc, and West, George, *The Electronic Day Trader,* copyright 1998 The McGraw-Hill Companies, Inc., page 32.

cific plan and following closely to it with discipline is gambling. Additionally, knowing when not to trade is also a step toward success. At times the Level II screen or the market offers no clarity, and when that is the case, walk away. The next chapter will cover some of these issues.

CHAPTER **6**

DEFINING YOUR E-DAT STYLE

B efore climbing into the cockpit of one of the most awesome
trading systems ever developed, you need to know a lot
about yourself and how you plan to use E-DAT. You must
understand your mindset and your missions. As you read this chapter, begin to consider how you plan to use E-DAT. Ask yourself
which style suits your personality and what you want to get out of
the system. Then, when you get to Chapters 7, 8, and 9, on trading
strategies, you'll have a better idea of which styles suit your special
needs.

I classify traders in two ways: The first is by the type of trading
they do, and the second is the duration of their trades, or their time
horizons. You will have to know your risk tolerance, time schedule,
and appetite for the market. Such an understanding will be your
beginning point, but always remember, trading like most activities is
a journey not a destination.

You will never know all there is to know, but the journey is
filled with excitement, victory, pain, and hard work. Waiting to learn
it all before you begin to trade will not work. No one has all the
answers. Because the market is so dynamic and prone to change, the

only real foundation to work from is understanding the psychology of the market. I have seen good companies lose value due to negative market sentiment, and weak companies trade at 100+ P/E ratios due to overreactions to news. Both are so because of psychology.

To learn this business, you need to pull the trigger. You need to interact with the market until you become the market. You must trade enough to trust your skill and knowledge. If you do not trade enough you will never develop the rhythm or discipline to be successful.

RISK TOLERANCE

In the Introduction, I talked about the electronic scalpers, or electronic day traders. These traders simply go wherever the action is, trading in any stock in motion. They trade more by instinct than anything else. You'll hear scalpers say, "I could smell that move coming," or "I could feel a retracement coming in my bones." They trade so fast and cover so many stocks that there is no time to do much analysis. Some do have certain analysis tools they consult, but once the opening bell rings, they run on 100-octane adrenaline.

The industry classifies them as heavy traders, meaning they do high-volume trading with a low profit margin per trade. An aggressive scalper might do as many as 100 to 200 trades a day looking for an average gross profit per trade of ¼ point. They are electronic day traders and never take positions home after the closing bell. Scalpers are action junkies and must always have a trade in the works. Their major flaw is overtrading. Because of the volume they do, they develop intuition and very keen instinct regarding market sentiment faster than any other style. I don't suggest starting with this style.

Some traders become gurus. They know one stock like most people know their spouse. Ask them what earnings were for the last decade and you'll get chapter and verse. If you want to see a chart of the stock's price activity for the last two days or years, they can draw one from memory. They can tell you what the officers have for breakfast on Fridays. The company, its products, industry, past, present, future—all available for the asking. More importantly for E-DAT, they know all the trading secrets and moves of the market makers in that particular stock. They patiently wait for trading opportunities and can make a living just knowing this one company.

Many of the decisions you make regarding what sectors you will focus in, what stocks within the sector, and how many stocks you will trade are very much dependent on your personality. Many traders will catch the rhythm of a particular company and hang on for all it is worth, while the electronic scalper seems to suffer from attention deficit disorder (ADD)! Your personality will determine more of this than anything else. Where do you find excitement, where do you get bored quickly, etc., are all factors that should be considered when determining where you will begin as an E-DAT. Once you feel your area of specialization is determined, what market input will you plug into your brain?

Do technical studies excite you, or do you like the street trader inside you that reads market momentum from a Level II? Perhaps you will study fundamentals, such as price earnings ratios (P/E) and book value. The point is, you can't serve many masters. You will need to commit to a discipline of trading and become absorbed by it, much like the young pre-med student who chooses neurology over proctology! You cannot serve all specialties in trading.

With all that considered, one common denominator that all studies will agree with is that electronic direct access trading is the cleanest, fastest, and best form of execution on the planet. Therefore, it is a must to compete effectively with the professionals.

TIME SCHEDULE

Your next consideration is determining the trading time frame that is most comfortable for you. For example, even scalpers and day traders tend to have definable patterns. Some hold positions for 1 to 20 minutes. Others for periods up to an hour, and some will keep trades several hours. Much depends on the exchanges they trade. The NASDAQ lends itself to the shortest of time frames. The study on the SOES bandits by Harris and Schultz mentioned in Chapter 7, suggests two minutes might be the top holding period for a NAS-DAQ momentum trade. The NYSE, with its more orderly markets overseen by a specialist, generally requires more time for trades to ripen.

The group of traders I refer to as swing, or short-term, traders have a trading time span of one to five days and are heavy users of technical analysis. As a rule, they avoid holding trades over weekends. Buy on Monday or Tuesday and close by Friday—this is their modus operandi. Personally, I like the idea of not having to think about my positions on days the market in not open. In the past when I carried many overnight positions, I would sleep like a baby, up every hour or so, sobbing and crying. Electronic trading is about being swift and decisive, right or wrong decisions are acted upon very quickly regardless of the result. I tell our traders all the time, "Do not try to squeeze all the juice out of the orange." In other words, don't expect to buy bottoms and sell tops. It is not realistic.

I also see some good electronic traders I call position, or inter-mediate-term, traders. They buy and hold for up to 10 days. These are usually technical analysts following systems or watching certain indicators that they have learned to rely on, such as pattern recognition. Others are serious fundamentalists. What they seem to particularly like about electronic trading is the power of routing their orders to buy when the market makers begin buying. I also see some fundamental position traders who find that multiple-day holds just long enough to get the full impact of key financial news, like a merger, yet not so long as to get them in trouble. They get out while others are still buying and monitor this on their Level II.

Those who trade for more than 10 days and less than 30 I consider to be active investors. They are quite similar to the position traders, but with longer time horizons. This is often a reflection of the analytic tools they use. Some technical indicators simply take longer to develop.

The last group is the classic stock investor or the buy 'n' hold traders. They do extensive research and then marry a position—for better or worse, profit or loss do us part. But like all too many marriages these days, they part long before death. These traders like E-DAT for two reasons. First, they can get into a position fast and at a much better price than if they went through a traditional broker. By using an E-DAT broker or doing it themselves, they can often shave an ⅛ or ¼ point from the price of the stock by working the outside market. This may not be a big deal in a long-term trade, but it pays for those pesky commissions. Think of it from a net-profit stand-point. Saving eighths and quarters over a year's time could mean a difference of between 23 and 30 percent return on investment, depending on trading volume. The second reason they are E-DAT fans is the divorce aspects of trading. If for whatever reason they lose faith in any of their positions, they can make it vanish in a mouse click. These traders do not necessarily need access to the Level II screen. They can get by with a much more economical Level I screen, which is available now from some E-DAT brokerage firms complete with an excellent trading software platform.

MARKET APPETITE

In order to trade in the markets two of the most important attributes you can possess is your passion for the market and the perception of yourself as a trader.

Without passion, don't waste your time or your money because you will lose both. You must love to walk, talk, think, and study market theory if you will develop as a successful trader. What you feed your mind, and how often, will mold your attitude of the market. But it all starts with passion, not greed.

As far as perception goes, I can't think of a better example of what helped me shape my own attitude of trading than a party I was invited to on top of Breckenridge Mountain during ski season. It was the close of the season, and several professionals of all kinds were present and we began to introduce ourselves and our professions. One gentleman was proud to introduce himself as a surgeon, and another as a pilot. When I told people I traded for a living, all eyes focused on me with a myriad of questions. I realized then the power of what I was fortunate to have. So many people who have studied and worked hard are not doing what they love or have the freedom to control their own destiny. Some are servants to a pager like so many doctors on call. Others need to be at work to produce revenue at all times. Traders can turn on the faucet whenever they want to and take profits out of the market with the sole requirement of skill. To me, that is very powerful and exciting. To others, it is one of the most exciting businesses there is, and it seems that today everyone wants in the game.

Forester Research did a study and predicts that by the year 2002, over 14 million people in America will be trading on-line, making this business the biggest thing since the Industrial Revolution. Many will lose big time, others will thrive, and the defining element will be who will demonstrate discipline and skill and who will treat the market like a casino. The market is not a casino. It is a thinking person's game that requires hard work and a solid understanding of the psychology of the market.

Now let's talk more about the psychology of trading electronically. Some of the information in this chapter draws on people such as Tony Robbins, Zig Zeigler, and Steven Covey. That is because psychology is often the foundation of these motivational speakers. They tell us things we usually already know, but say it in such a way that it motivates us to act. Plus they usually say it better than we can. Does that make them smarter than we are? Only if they practice what they teach and we don't. The reality is, the entire trading package comes down to the following parts:

- Knowledge
- Confidence
- The ability to act
- The willingness to keep learning
- The ability to accept failure and responsibility

Reading this book is a good start to gaining knowledge. After that, I recommend some classroom instruction, followed by time on an E-DAT simulator. If you have the knowledge, you gain the confidence and lose the fear. And if that is true, you will then be like the student who studied extra hard for the final exam and can't wait to take the test (ability to act). You will get great results due to your knowledge, confidence, and ability to take action. These results bring you what you went after, and you will have fun doing it. Success will inspire you to continue to learn to enhance your E-DAT skills. It all sounds pretty good, doesn't it? It sounds right because we have been there! I have felt success and, I suspect, you have as well—or you could not afford to trade. So what stops most people? The answer is the last item on the list above.

Most people have never learned to accept responsibility for failure. They tend to ignore it and move on to something else that makes them feel good, not bad. Guess what? Trading is going to make you feel bad at times. We all work hard to make our money, right? And because of that we associate some pain and pride with that hard work. Losing money at lightning speed is very difficult to handle.

What you have learned up to this point is not worth a teenie on a 100-lot trade if you cannot learn to handle the losses. Losses are part of the game, just as interceptions are for John Elway or your favorite quarterback. If you let your losing trades shape your opinions of yourself in terms of your trading ability, the market becomes a 1500-mile-per-hour jet totally out of trim and taking you down with it.

Attitude, in my opinion, is hard to teach and I am not going to try. If you think you need more help, read the book I referenced earlier, *Learned Optimism,* and always do the following:

- Take responsibility for your own trades.
- Do not hold losers. Admit you are wrong and be done with it.
- Do not beat yourself up when you are wrong. This is not so easy to do when losses amount to thousands of dollars, but it must be done. We need to get up again after we have fallen.
- Prepare to do battle another day.

These are the marks of a successful E-DAT trader. Will you pay the true price? Or do you just like the idea of trading more than doing it? I have met many people who have a stock-trading system in their homes, right next to their home theaters. They show it to their friends so they look smart. Most of these people never make it, because they want to feel like a trader more than they want to be a trader. They seem to be more hungry for the recognition than for financial gain.

Someone once asked me if I realized how brash that sounds. I said I do, but you did not buy this book to be pampered. This is a challenging business, and it is made more interesting by its speed and excitement. Consider what I am telling you as "tough love." If you really want to make it, and you succeed, it is your success, not anyone else's. Conversely, if you fail, you own that as well. No one can give you the attitude necessary to be a successful trader: "Your attitude determines your altitude!"

I would like to talk about fear and reinforcement for a moment, two compelling arguments that psychologists have argued for years. In the market, fear rears its ugly head a number of ways. One example would be the boom/bust theory. The fear is on both sides: the fear of missing the boom while it is occurring, and the fear of being in the market while the bust is present.

A second example comes in the form of a question. If you had one hand in a vise under great pressure and with the other hand you could reach out and grab the most exciting tool you could ever imagine—which hand would you move first? Or let's put it another way, which would motivate you to action first?

I think most of us would want to relieve the pain first, before reaching for the valuable tool. Speculating in the stock market can often elicit similar patterns in decision making, while not as severe. Fear occurs when you have entered a trade and it goes against you, often referred to in the industry as "the heat." The fear associated with taking the loss overwhelms you to stay in the trade because of a very powerful four-letter word (settle down! not that word) . . . *hope!* Your hope that it will come back, leads you down a road you wish you had gotten off sooner. When you look again, you experience the pain associated with a losing trade. At the early stage, it is tolerable. But as the bleeding continues, it becomes intolerable at some point.

Some traders never let go and the trade goes to the point where your brokerage firm needs to wake you up with a margin call! The point is, fear can keep you out of the market when you should be in, due to a lack of confidence, and it can keep you in when you should be out. Quite the irony, isn't it? The cliché "The road to hell is paved with good intentions" comes to mind.

Reinforcement issues exist as well, especially when it relates to discipline and doing the right thing when the heat is on. For example, a trade is moving against you. You cover immediately, which is the right thing to do. The theory of positive reinforcement is still elusive at that moment because in the trader's mind, he or she still realizes the loss. This is hard to comprehend because of our conditioning. When we do the right things, we expect to receive positive reinforcement.

Trading doesn't always pay that dividend. The benefits can come perhaps a day later, when the trade that was dumped, is now down a few more points. Then you can feel good about it. The point is that a trader needs to develop somewhat of a contrarian view of the market in terms of not just trading strategies but also human conditioning, how to feel good about a losing trade. Losing is as much a part of trading as strikeouts are in baseball. Learn to deal with them quickly and positively.

People often hear me talk about the "emotional bank account," and I thought of this concept while cold calling early on in my career. Most of us have been taught to associate success with unrealistic results, such as selling our product the first time in front of the prospect, or making a good trade the first few times at bat. Emotionally we have already set ourselves up for a fall because in our minds we believe we should achieve the successful result, and when it does not occur, it elicits an "emotional withdrawal" from our bank account. Enough of those, a salesperson stops calling, and a trader stops trading by becoming emotionally bankrupt!

I would tell you not to expect the results to come that easy and to learn to recognize a good loss. Expect them; they are great to learn from, and you won't succeed unless you step into the batter's box and get hit with a few pitches. By not expecting too much too fast, your emotional side is protected, and when losses are cut fast, they can actually become emotional deposits, not to mention what they can do for your financial bank account, when positions run away due to poor discipline.

The moral is, forget fear and overcome it with cold, calculated decisions. Truly believe that there is such a thing as a good loss, such as when a position rolls against you, and you cut your losses quickly. The exception would be if you are looking for the slight "pullback" or "headfake," the kind of fakeout the market makers will often throw at you. Here you must have the confidence to stay with the trade because you recognize the pattern. Keep in mind this type of trading elevates the risk factors.

The stock market is psychology in action. It is people just like you making guesses as to the impact of supply and demand on prices. Some may use technical analysis while others read the Level II screen; it does not matter because it all comes down to their emotional reaction to price activity. Some are greedy, others cold logicians. Still others rely on superstition. I have seen traders who used the phases of the moon to pick stocks. No matter what, it is human psychology playing itself out in the bids and offers you will see on the Level II screen. How do you see yourself? That's the key. If you are confident and relaxed, you will do well. If you are not, you need to decide if you want to continue pursuing a trading career. If you do, go back to the list of what makes up a complete trading package. Then figure out what you are lacking and find a source to provide you with the missing ingredient.

Your attitude defines everything about you that makes you unique. It can also prevent you from achieving success because it is here that the obstacles to successful trading are buried. Your attitude will create a self-fulfilling prophecy.

The key to fighting fear is knowledge, and it will give you the confidence to take action! Confidence about your knowledge replaces fear. Baseline market knowledge can be obtained by attending a good stock-trading school before you begin to trade. You can choose to pay for education once or to pay for ignorance over a lifetime.

The strategies covered in the next chapter are based on market psychology and are designed to take advantage of how the market, as a whole, reacts and responds. How well you can take advantage of it depends not only on your skill as a trader but also on your confidence and ability to take action—and this is tied to your tolerance to risk and uncertainty. If you need some development in these areas, perhaps you need to do a "fire walk" with Tony Robbins or learn how to skydive, but if overcoming fear is a problem for you, trading may be as well.

Finally, how will you handle yourself when you are in a trade opportunity without any clear picture of what the outcome will be? A technique I teach is visualization. You picture in your mind exactly how you expect a trade to take place. If it does not follow your script, you close it out immediately.

As a new trader it's crucial that you "paper" or practice trading as much as necessary to understand how to identify the moves and how to get in and out of positions. But to develop trading skills, it is important to trade as often as possible. Simulation trading is no substitute for experience, but it can put mind and hand in concert, which is very important in E-DAT.

In electronic trading, paper trading means working on a simulator, preferably one using a live price feed. A simulator is a trading platform that exactly duplicates the trading software you will be using, only the trades never enter the market. You win or lose cyber dollars. Your trades are diverted and filled by a computer model of markets based on real-time price activity, which gives you a feeling for E-DAT. The reason I stress this approach is that it takes some time to just get comfortable with the software. You must be able to point and click fast and accurately. When you spot an opportunity or need to cut a loss in its infancy, you do not want to have to ask someone what to do or where to point the mouse. You must react almost intuitively, like a fighter pilot locking on a target.

Let's just talk through some typical situations you will face. For example, a news event occurs prompting a reaction in the price of a stock you are tracking. Although yesterday's news, this type of reaction and overreaction occurs regularly and can be traded over and over again because it is just an example of what regularly occurs, or of human nature as it manifests itself in the stock market. People change, but seldom!

When Microsoft was about to introduce Windows 98, electronic traders who were astute and in front of a real-time Level II system would have seen exactly what I have been speaking about. Namely, psychology and pure supply versus demand at work. Together, they revealed the public's reaction and where the market-making community was going.

On the Level II screen for a solid 10 days, I watched major firms like Goldman Sachs (GSCO), Morgan Stanley (MSCO), Merrill Lynch (MLCO) and others buy up MSFT. The whole process started when the stock was trading at around $86 and continued right up until the product was released. The buying frenzy was clear and happened before the release date of the product as MSFT stock ran up to $116 per share, an obvious overreaction.

The public waited for the release date to buy the stock. By then it was too late. Many novice investors bought on broker recommendations after the product was released, which was too late. The professional E-DAT traders and market makers already bought the stock on the anticipation of the release and sold it as the release date of the product approached. They sold into the buying strength of the public.

E-DAT traders should have sold the stock the day Windows 98 was released, even though the stock did continue to rise. The reaction prior to the release was predictable by watching the market makers, on the Level II screen, buy the stock in huge quantities. The continued upward trend of the stock after the release was not as predictable and would be classified as the chaos stage. Having the electronic capability to watch the buying sentiment prior to the release date was critical. It was possible to measure the professional money flow versus the public's reaction, which provided liquidity to the selling professionals.

This is an example of how technology, electronics data, lightning-fast execution, psychology, and an understanding of public reaction can be combined to make successful trades in the electronic trading world.

A final point on this real-life example, the astute E-DAT trader would not try to sell the MSFT high, which was $116. This is because this move occurred after the release date. Waiting too long is extremely risky and unpredictable. The game plan is to profit and move on to a new play. Avoid chaos, which tends to be associated with the public's reaction.

Do not wait for the obvious, trade ahead of news and events. An electronic real-time trading platform gives you the ability to read the reaction and ticker tape of where the money flow is, ahead of the actual event. You catch the wave on the way up! Buy rumor; sell fact.

ALL SHIPS RISE WITH THE TIDE

We have seen the effects of strikes, banking scares, global economic crises, microchip competition, and many other events that seem to shape sectors of the market from both the upside and the downside.

When news rocks a stock or a specific event affects an industry, the ripple effect caused by the news will shake up the stocks within that sector. When the news is strong, many corporations will reap the benefit, even when they are not the direct recipient of the news. Often the chaos of the news in the specific stock is too difficult to trade and too risky because of possible leaks of the news before the announcements, or there is just too much money flowing in both directions, both in and out of the stock, to trade it with confidence.

Here is a good example. When Daimler-Benz first announced its intention to merge with Chrysler, the other stocks in that industry sector also had good moves, although not nearly as dramatic. Ford went up, as did General Motors. When there is takeover talk or merger mania between banks and brokerage firms, all these types of firms react. So it's important to note that news about a particular stock can affect all of the stocks in the same group to some extent. When the tide rises, all the ships in the harbor rise. The companies in the news move on rumors, but the ancillary companies move for a short time after the news and can be the smartest plays. See Figure 6-1.

These strategies really are timeless. They have been used in professional circles for many years. While the specific examples change, the principles remain constant.

FIGURE 6-1 *News events that move a stock's price are surprises. You must be prepared to respond to them almost instinctively. The top diagram shows how a stock might respond to positive news. The bottom diagram shows a possible response to negative news. Both situations offer the astute trader some interesting opportunities.*

News-Driven Price Patterns

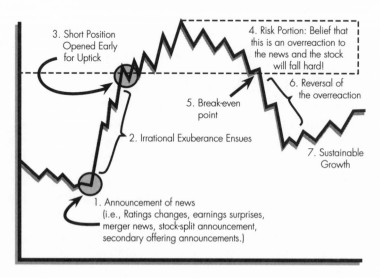

3. Short Position Opened Early for Uptick

4. Risk Portion: Belief that this is an overreaction to the news and the stock will fall hard!

6. Reversal of the overreaction

5. Break-even point

2. Irrational Exuberance Ensues

7. Sustainable Growth

1. Announcement of news (i.e., Ratings changes, earnings surprises, merger news, stock-split announcement, secondary offering announcements.)

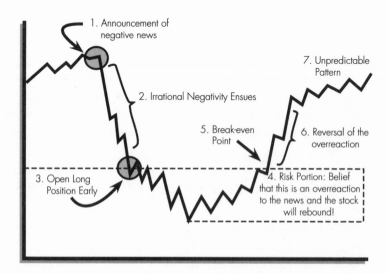

1. Announcement of negative news

7. Unpredictable Pattern

2. Irrational Negativity Ensues

5. Break-even Point

6. Reversal of the overreaction

3. Open Long Position Early

4. Risk Portion: Belief that this is an overreaction to the news and the stock will rebound!

LEVEL II AND THE MEDIA

When you have electronic access to the market in real time and a Level II screen, discovering what the market makers are doing with news prior to its becoming public is one of the hottest games on the street. The public becomes the liquidity for the E-DAT trader when patience, keen observation, and the ability to act come together before the news reaches the general public. The ability to act means to move into positions before they are known and even shorting them when they become known if an overreaction occurs, based on good news. Or short anticipated bad news before it is known, then buy the weakness after it becomes known. Follow this psychology, and you will be well on your way to becoming a successful trader.

Don't be too concerned that this information will influence the market in a way that will change these concepts. They have been used by the professionals for years and will continue to be productive. Human nature is difficult to change. The public will continue to wait to have the facts before reacting. So fire up your NASDAQ Level II system and watch the money flow between the pros and the public. Then trade on a simulator to reinforce your ability to read this consensus and build confidence. In the next chapter (7), I will talk about specific E-DAT strategies for both listed and NASDAQ issues.

CHAPTER

7

TRADING STRATEGIES AND LIGHTING-UP YOUR WEAPONS SYSTEMS

A s fighter pilots burn classroom time learning the basic tactics of air-to-air and air-to-ground warfare, they get antsy to actually get into their Tomcats and try out all they have learned. There is nothing like locking onto a live target to raise the adrenaline. Although I cannot set you up to trade via this book, I now want to teach you some of the actual tactics you can use when you do go "live."

Let me start at the beginning, the time of the famous SOES bandits. The first individual traders to use the SOES were called bandits by the industry because they "stole" the spread from the industry insiders, specifically market makers. They could do this in the early days of electronic trading (not so long ago) because SOES was so powerful. As you know, market makers must provide a two-sided market. The bandits could see that the spreads were too wide, and they would simply lift an offer (to buy) or hit a bid (to sell) and market makers had to honor the SOES order. As the SOES orders took out the supply on the offer, market makers would not refresh and the stock would move up to the next level.

Here is how they did it. NASDAQ stocks are constantly in motion with plenty of small moves up and down. Bandettos would lock onto the Level II market-making screen for a particular stock they knew was very volatile. The SOES bandits would SOES a market maker, who many times would withdraw its bid or offer. This diminished or increased the supply of that particular stock thus lowering or increasing the price. The bandits would then offset their positions on Select-Net or SOES an eighth- or a quarter-point higher. They could count on an easy ⅛- or ¼-point profit. Market makers don't make it that easy today. They stay at the bid or ask, which forces traders to truly read supply and demand activities. In short, the SOES bandits forced the market to get more efficient, and for this they deserve a lot of credit.

These tactics worked like a charm for a long time and really made the insiders angry, because they believed they owned the spread. The bandits were taking money from the insiders or market makers—they were the new version of Robin Hood and His Merry Band. As a result of their efforts and several SEC investigations, new trading rules that have been enacted, your ability to compete with the professional trading community has been enhanced even more.

Pure SOES trading still works in some cases, but not as often. It is simply too well known by the market makers. Now they often refuse to be SOESed out or to leave their quoted market. Additionally, the rule changes and narrow spreads have created new opportunities. The problem is there are now thousands of active SOES traders competing with you to SOES that last offer. This impedes your ability to execute that way. It's important to note that most SOES traders only SOES on a limit, which is a fading price. Therefore, the SOES traders in this play have zero demand at the next level. That is why more market makers refuse to revise their quote to the next level.

This question of not being able now to emulate the SOES bandits brings up a very important point about common sense and why I prefer not to be too literal. The concept behind the theory of supply and demand is really what you need to learn. If you understand that and incorporate it into your thinking about the market, many opportunities present themselves, as opposed to your trying to emulate literal trading strategies. Another cliché I think about a lot is, "Give a man a fish and feed him for a day. Teach him to fish and feed him for a lifetime."

I really want you to understand how to think like the market makers, so you approach the market the way they do. The strategies will change, but the psychology behind the markets will remain. That is more important to learn, than step-by-step explanations of tactics.

THE AX

As in ordinary life, some people, and even businesses, are too busy to play games, while others waste time and energy creating new angles to work the system. Market makers seem to take on the same personalities.

Many firms simply have too much order flow or too large a customer base of institutional clients to play around with their quotes on a Level II screen or on any other system NASDAQ may incorporate in the future. These firms need to get their orders filled for their customers and tend to be straightforward. When they need to buy stock, they show themselves as net buyers by spending more time on the bid than the offer, trading higher volume. For example, GSCO (Goldman Sachs) wants to buy 1,000,000 shares for a large customer, such as a pension fund. Astute traders see that throughout the day GSCO is buying up the stock and that as a result of the bidding, the stock moves higher. This is known as the *market impact cost,* or MIC. Does this mean that GSCO will just sit on the bid all day, and buy through SelectNet and InstiNet with other firms at offer prices? No. GSCO wants to hide this order, as best it can. But the level of transparency on the Level II, real-time screen shows you that GSCO is the "ax." The "ax" is the dominant market maker in a specific stock. At a given time, there will be other times GSCO is not dominant, and then not an ax.

Other market makers (smaller firms) will try and fake you out and not be as easy to read. I try to ignore them since they tend to be smaller firms who are rarely the "ax." They try to read market sentiment and make things happen so that they can buy someone else's weakness or panic and sell into strength. Therefore, these firms often play games in an attempt to convince you that it is the ax, but it really isn't. A trained eye will tell who is the real ax and who is not. Shadowing these firms makes it difficult to make money because of the headfakes and games. Therefore, I suggest that you obtain proper training to find out who the players are and who typically are true axes and who are phonies.

There are several strategies that work well once you understand who the market makers are and what their trading patterns are. I like the concept of shadowing the ax because while the entire world is trying to see the forest from the trees and figure out what the market is doing, I am in the woods moving in and out of trades out of sight, like a sniper. There are times when you want a broad perspective of the market, but not with this strategy.

SHADOWING THE AX

One of the most reliable strategies for the electronic trader to master is called *shadowing*. A market maker shows dominance in a stock. It is continually buying stock while other market makers are leaving the current bid on the Level II screen. This market maker displays an insatiable appetite for the stock and continues to buy at the quoted bid or inside bid or high bid. Other traders, especially the traditional SOES traders, panic because the other market makers are leaving the current high bid, which would appear to show a contracting market or diminishing demand. As you know, when demand starts to contract, supply tends to increase and the price falls. Most SOES traders will see this and immediately hit the bid and sell out their longs, hence creating liquidity for the ax market maker, that is, sitting at that bid to buy up the weakness.

This market maker is buying as the sellers are rushing out of what appears to be a contracting market. But, the market maker's refusal to leave that bid tells the trained trader that this market maker has a good size order to fill or some other need for the stock. Your move is to shadow this market maker. You will be filled very quickly because panicking sellers are hitting the bid or selling as fast as they can. This is the concept of buying weakness. Soon other traders and market makers will realize the current bid is going to stand. When this occurs, demand will grow at the current bid and eventually a higher bid becomes the new inside bid. You will be sitting there pretty happy at that point letting the profits run until the supply on the offer side begins to build.

Always remember the foundation of economic theory. When supply expands, demand tends to contract and so do prices. When supply contracts, demand increases and so do prices. The Level II screen is like having a virtual seat on the exchange. You are in the middle of pure capitalism—pure supply and demand. If a market maker is showing inordinate demand for a stock, shadow that market maker and do the same thing it does. Buy when it buys; sell when it sells.

Here is an example. If MLCO (Merrill Lynch) wants to buy ASND (Ascend Communications, Inc.), it will bid high. The market is 45 bid × 45⅛ offered. MLCO suddenly bids 45⅟₁₆ for the stock and remains there. After several trades, sellers of all kinds hit MLCO at the bid. Then MLCO leaves the bid and doesn't even do anything obvious like join the offer. It simply pulls its bid to avoid buying any more. Minutes later MLCO comes back to buy at the current bid or even higher. It is the leader or the ax. As MLCO continues to do this without ever selling, you should realize it isn't a seller, but a net buyer. It wants to buy quietly and not show its hand to the world.

The next time MLCO joins the bid or goes high bid, you follow the leader and buy with it. If it pulls the bid, but does not join the offer, don't be so inclined to sell or panic. It will come and go often. Think of MLCO as a bird taking a few crumbs at a time. When it feels its confidentiality is breached, it will leave, only to come back a few minutes later to take some more crumbs. You shadow these moves.

When MLCO stops going to the bid or joins an offer, sell the stock and take a profit. The process of MLCO buying the stock over a period of time causes the stock to go up. It won't be just because MLCO is buying. Many other traders who are watching this dance will join the bid when MLCO does. Many will also sell too soon, when MLCO leaves to take a breather. If you are not patient enough to realize the ax will be back to buy more, you may also leave too early. Be patient, this will help you realize more profit as the stock slowly moves higher and save commission by not constantly entering and exiting the market, like traditional SOES traders. When MLCO no longer looks like a buyer, you sell out.

Remember some moves are more obvious than others. Going high bid is more dramatic than jumping on the bid, but both are bullish. Leaving the bid to go low offer is a strong sell indication, while leaving the bid temporarily only to come back to the bid, isn't. The more you can understand these nuances, the more your radar will tune in on the nature of market makers and the more you will make intuitive decisions as opposed to trying to implement current day strategies that will change and become obsolete.

TRADING IPOs AND SECONDARY OFFERINGS

Trading IPOs and secondary stock offerings are tricky business. If you can get an allocation of stock of an IPO, you probably do not want it. Here is why.

The way to the hearts of underwriters and firms that are part of a syndicate or selling group is through the institutional desk. Customers who can pass enough trade volume through this desk will get "valued client status" (VCS), similar to being a VIP. These are the customers who trade enough volume to generate enough commissions for the firm to allocate IPO shares to them. Most IPOs go up from the POP (public offering price) on the day the shares hit the secondary market; thus those with VCS can flip the IPO shares on day one for a nice profit. Everyone wants IPOs allotted to them. If you do not have VCS and get an allocation, the stock is probably a dog.

Now, you are probably asking, "Why do I need this information if I can't get an allocation of the IPO I want?" The reason has more to do with secondary offerings.

Secondary offerings are offerings of additional shares of stock by public companies seeking to raise additional capital. This offering is generally a symptom of a strong company, not a weak one. Companies expand in bullish times, particularly if interest rates are low, products are selling well, etc. Companies often need to expand to meet growing demand. Because these corporations tend to be entrepreneurial in spirit, they wish to expand faster than the earnings of the company allow. Thus a secondary offering is called for.

Never buy secondary offerings in weak markets or such offerings from companies without earnings. These corporations are raising capital for the wrong reason, i.e., survival rather than continued success.

Look for strength in the offering. This is similar to buying on a Sonic Boom signal, after a breakout and the first pullback. You do not want to buy the secondary offerings without a positive move because there may be some unusual price activity and these offerings usually perform poorly. In other words, if the stock ASND (Ascend Communications, Inc.) makes a secondary offering and the underwriters, along with its selling group, do not do a great job, the small demand depresses the issues after the offering. Therefore, you, as the owner of 2000 shares, will probably see a retracement once this offering starts trading. Conversely, if the offering goes off well and the stock experiences a positive move of at least a quarter point after the issue, buy it.

Be ready to sell the stock quickly, within one to three days maximum, because the positive emotion associated with the offering is usually short-lived. Additionally, remember the concept of "stabilization." This is where the underwriting firm attempts to prop up or support the stock after an offering by bidding the stock at a average price level equal to the strongest bid in the market. The selling groups and underwriters do not want the stock to fall below the offering price because they sold it to their best customers. That would not make them happy and could cost the firm future business. For all these reasons, the stocks that open by at least a quarter point are usually good buys in the secondary market, but should also be closed out quickly as well. Remember, we are talking about fast, short-term plays. If reaction appears weak after you get long, exercise discipline and cut your loss.

If the stock continues to rise, be ready to sell the stock on strength, or while it appears still strong to ensure liquidity. Remember, do not try to pick tops and buy bottoms. You must sell when others are buying. Think of these secondary issues as a book on *The New York Times* best sellers list. It attracts a lot of attention for a little while, but once the demand has been met, best sellers lose steam fast and disappear from the public eye. You can find a list of IPOs and secondary offerings in the following Web sites and publications:

Firstcall.com

Zacks.com

Barron's

Investor's Business Daily

TRADING LISTED SECURITIES

The strategies for trading listed securities are a little different than for NASDAQ stocks. The premise of trying to trade like a NYSE specialist, who is often doing the opposite of what a trader might be doing, can be complicated. Sometimes, for example, when you trade, you buy strength and sell weakness; other times you will do the opposite as indicated earlier. But when trading listed securities (always assume NYSE), you need to pay close attention as well as knowing the companies fundamentally. Before we look at a few strategies, one rule I teach and follow is that I momentum trade only listed stocks that I like and believe to be strong companies. Let's explore a few scenarios:

• The stock CPQ (Compact Computer, Inc.) is trading and showing strength over the time horizon you are measuring and charting. A relative strength reading (published in

Investor's Business Daily) of 95 or higher is considered strong. As CPQ trades higher, you notice on your Level II that CPQ is 85 × 85¼, 5000 × 2000. This tells you there is a buyer for 5000 CPQ. If no sellers come out to sell at 85, this is a strong indication the price is not good enough. Then the market changes to 85⅛ × 85⅜, 5000 × 2000. You come to the conclusion the buyer wants it badly and the specialist is pushing the price higher to find a seller. This increase in the bid shows you the demand is high for this stock. Therefore, you will lift the offer and buy the stock at the offer price of 85⅜. This creates more strength for the stock because you took some of the 85⅜ supply that was for sale. If you are right, decreasing the supply, coupled with the demand at 85⅛, should drive the stock higher and force the buyer of those 5000 shares to pay even more, perhaps lift the offer like you did. This can certainly drive the stock up a few price levels and secure you a tidy little profit. This is called "trading to size," meaning that the demand size of the bid at 5000 tells you to pay a little higher than the bid. Being the bidder at 5000 means someone really wants the stock. All you did was trade ahead of the demand.

- It is important to mention a few other scenarios. Often a buyer in listed stock will not want to show his intentions to the market. Therefore, in the example, the market on CPQ shows more sellers than buyers, such as CPQ 85 × 85¼, 2000 × 10,000. At face value, the stock looks weak. If the Time and Sales screen shows that 3000 shares just traded at the bid and the bid is not reduced, or it is even increased, this is a sign that the stock could move higher. The buy that took place was filled from the 10,000 available. Once the remaining 7000 shares are taken, the seller is all done and should create a net buying situation to drive the stock higher, because the weakness is gone, which allows the buyers to come in.

- Another point worth exploring regarding listed trading is the opportunity to see "price improvement" on market

orders placed on the SuperDot system. Price improvement
is available many times when the specialist is resolving
imbalances with supply and demand. For example, if the
current market in CPQ is 85 × 85¼ 1000 × 10,000, the specialist who receives a market order bidding for 1000 shares,
may do what is called "stop" the stock. This would simply
mean that instead of filling the buyer at 85¼ (the seller's
price), the specialist may stop the stock and guarantee that
the buyer will receive the 85¼, but then bid the 1000 shares
at 85⅛ to narrow the spread and make a more efficient market. The current market would then be 85⅛ × 85¼ 1000 ×
10,000. If a seller at 85¼ hits the new bid, the buyer is
receiving an improved price at 85⅛ instead of paying 85¼.
The current market would then change, indicating a
reduced volume for sale on the offer, and indicating the
stock may be weak, since the seller took less for the stock.

This practice is seen quite often on the SuperDot system
and affords traders the opportunity to use a market order
with confidence.

It isn't always easy to see these moves developing. It takes time
to develop tape-reading skills, but in time you will see these plays. It
will be blatantly obvious and you will know exactly what to do without hesitation. Training your instincts to react is one of the many
keys to profitable trading. Your attitude is also critical. It often takes
perseverance to continue to trade and learn the idiosyncrasies of the
NASDAQ compared to the NYSE.

On the NASDAQ, you have market makers to contend with
who are negotiating bids and asks, competing against each other,
as well as against you. And then there are the NYSE specialists,
who are just as elusive—often trading contrary to the market. Keep
focused on the rewards you can expect when you learn to trade
like a professional. It takes time and practice to see, but the technology that exists today can help you learn to trade just as the specialist does on the floor, but in cyber space. When you watch the

market move as a result of these scenarios, the light bulb will go off, and once you have the knowledge, no one will ever take it away from you!

Chapter 8 will show you how not to lose your money with news-driven events, once you know that, profits will come like an "invisible hand," pushing you to successful trades.

CHAPTER 8

EARNINGS

Perfecting your trading skills will be like learning to dogfight. Moreover, the primary weapon system of both the fighter pilot and the E-DAT trader is the computer. One tried-and-true method of preparing for the challenge of E-DAT is planning for a very fertile opportunity that repeatedly presents itself, the earnings play.

BUY RUMOR, SELL FACT

The reaction of a stock's price to earnings announcements is an area that offers you substantial trading opportunities. There are a number of important things to understand before digging into this often mis-understood and mistraded stock play.

Trading on earnings reports offers at least three distinct trading opportunities. As short-term traders it is important to remember that you want to minimize your exposure as much as possible. Before you consider trading strategies, you need some basic knowledge about earnings.

First, the companies that report earnings do not "miss their number" because it really isn't their number at all. The number you see, flashed about in the financial news before an earnings report, is the average estimate of quarterly earnings made by the analysts who follow the stock. Professional analysts are generally Chartered Financial Analysts, and they rely heavily on "fundamental" analysis of the industries and companies. They also develop close relationships with officers and other key players and adjust their estimates based on feedback from their contacts. As the earnings announcement date draws nearer, analysts sometimes adjust their estimates. This puts them in a position to influence public opinion—and in turn the stock's price—on any given stock, depending on whether they are high or low on their estimates.

Perception is reality in the markets. How people perceive earnings reports and similar bits of information determines how they trade. Wall Street expects a certain reaction from the general investing public, and they usually get it. The public will react to things professional traders won't. This reaction from the public produces much of the liquidity for the professionals, and in order to help the reaction occur, a good bit of hype and news will be created on earnings. Because of the same reasons the average investor will react to a stock tip, they will certainly act on what they believe is a good source of news, e.g., television. My advice is not to walk away from stock tips . . . RUN. But the public often will not recognize such good advice. Think about it: If a person would commit their capital to a stock that was suggested to them from their friend's uncle who knows someone who works for this super company, that is going to make all that buy now rich. Wouldn't you think they would react to Mark Haynes on CNBC if he says earnings look good for Cisco next quarter?

The professionals count on the fact that the public will react. Unfortunately they want that reaction so that they can get on the other side of it, leaving the unsuspecting investor once again scratching his or her head in amazement when Cisco falls like a simonized safe after beating the Street's earnings consensus estimate.

The point is, both professionals and the public will buy and sell stock, but usually during different times and with very different results.

Earnings estimates are created and reported by multiple sources and an earnings consensus is the summary of these estimates. Brokerage firms and analysts from around the country will project what they feel earnings will be, and the average of these projections is referred to as the consensus estimate, which is what the media reports. The analysts, not the companies, create the expectation and the reaction that comes from the public. What is most important to understand is that no one really knows what the earnings will be until the day they are reported. Because of the time lapse between the anticipated earnings report and the actual event, it is just as important to understand that public opinion may be manipulated as it is to know that earnings reports do actually drive the market. Both of these provide you with excellent opportunities, as long as you don't listen to your friend's uncle!

Also keep in mind that the key is what is expected, not what you think may happen or what actually does happen. The markets make violent moves when something happens that is not expected, rather than when the expected happens. This is the earnings surprise that you have heard of, which is substantially different and a different play than when earnings expectations and actual results are fairly close.

If stock earnings are expected to be positive, the stock price tends to rise before the announcement. Then there is often a sell-off and profit-taking the day earnings are reported. If the expectations are not met or they are substantially higher than expected, that is when the real surprises occur.

To trade earnings profitably, you need to view them like a chess game and plan your strategy a few moves ahead. If you could always call the direction of the reaction correctly, trading stocks would be a snap and it wouldn't have any value because everyone would do it. And you would not need to devote much thought to make profitable trades.

Another point to understand is that earnings announcements are foreseeable events and the trading that takes place is based on the perception and hype surrounding them. Events that are sudden and unpredictable, such as upgrades, downgrades, or stock-split announcements, are different. The astute trader searches for price patterns to determine what the "Street" is thinking in terms of the trend or the directional bias, in order to take a position prior to the actual event. This is known as trading on expectation (see Figure 8-1).

FIGURE 8-1 *The earnings play is one of the most dependable stock plays. Be sure to have a good source of information regarding what the "whisper" number is.*

Earnings...Buy Rumor, Sell Fact

PLAY #1: Uncertainty Stage. Read the direction of the stock for approximately two days about seven days before the earnings report is due. Go LONG in this example.

PLAY #2: As the News Date draws closer, "whisper" earnings estimates begin to come out. Certainty begins to set in—sell your long position.

PLAY #3: Sell the stock short as the pros sell into amateur long orders. Buy in to cover your short before the close (you DO have the option to open a long position. See play #4).

PLAY #4: Buy at the close before earnings news released to play for an upside gap at the open. Note: This is VERY RISKY!

PLAY #5: Cover long position if you played #4. Sell the news short. Cover this short position within an hour or so (before noon).

The actual earnings figures are almost always reported after the close of the markets, usually just after 4:30 p.m. EST, but there are exceptions. Occasionally earnings are reported in the middle of the day. A few sources, which provide earnings calendars and estimates, are:

- *Barron's*
- *Investor's Business Daily*
- CNBC
- *The Nightly Business News* program on PBS
- Internet sites, such as:
    - stocktools.com
    - newsalert.com
    - bloomberg.com
    - streetwatch.com
    - firstcall.com

HOW TO TRADE EARNINGS ELECTRONICALLY

The Wall Street professionals do not wait for the news; instead, they trade ahead of it. Professionals look for money to flow into or out of the stock prior to the earning's reports. Then they join that trend long before the report comes out. The E-DAT traders, who can read the directional bias created by the smart money taking an early position, will reduce market risk greatly while increasing profit potential. The E-DAT traders will look for volume to build over the normal range of the stock, and then determine on which side of the market the volume is flowing. Is the money pouring in or out of the stocks? Results come from taking risks early and not waiting for the news to be actually reported. Investors who wait to buy stock based on news reports typically lose.

The Wall Street professionals and successful E-DAT traders take the risk by trading the stock long before the event. For example, if a positive earnings result is expected, the professionals will trade before the announcement during the uncertainty stage. The money flow of the buying professionals generally drives the stock higher 7 to 10 days before the actual figures are released. The amateurs wait for "certainty" or the actual earnings news to be released before taking action, which creates the perfect opportunity for the professional traders to sell out their longs and into the buying public. This is the reason why stocks often reverse their positive direction after the release of seemingly good news. The word "scapegoat" comes to mind.

As the professionals move much more money out of the market than the public can absorb, good stocks can "tank" on good news. For example, suppose Intel stock falls four points on the release of earnings even higher than the consensus estimated. The explanation is that Intel had already traded up seven or eight points on the expectation of good earnings news. The consensus in the stock was strong, represented by institutional money buying the stock, which helped push the price higher prior to the earnings announcement. When the earnings were finally released, the number was indeed positive, but the professionals drove the price down by selling the now overvalued stock to the amateurs rushing in to buy on the good news!

In this type of situation electronic trading capabilities can really pay off. For example, you can call up charts of Intel before, during, and after earnings reports. Learn how it reacted. What did it do 10 days prior to the last two reports that are similar to the one expected or anticipated by the industry insiders' predictions? Five days prior? The actual day of the earnings report? The day after? The week after? Once you get a good feel for what the professionals did in the past, you will understand what to do for the next earnings play. By following the real-time data and a Level II screen, you determine what the market makers are doing and the directional bias of the stock will generally confirm what you see the market maker doing early enough to realize the lowest risk, highest profit potential trade. You can predict entry and exit points, such as pullback areas and other patterns. Additionally, your electronic order-entry system gives you the ability to buy bids and save the spread, or place "resting" orders in at prices you believe to be the "actual" bid, based on your interpretation of the "ax."

In short, the professional money generally goes against the public, which lends credence to the industry cliché, "Buy rumors, sell facts." Of course, the opposite would be true for anticipated negative earnings reports as well.

THE WHISPER NUMBER

The "whisper number" is the unpublished number, among the analyst community, as to what their real expectation of a stock's earnings is. The analysts publish official estimates, which become known through the media. As the reporting day draws nearer, the whisper number isn't so quiet anymore. This is the number the public usually trades. As the earnings announcement date approaches, the analysts begin to unofficially hint at what they really think the earnings will be. As the whisper number becomes more known, more public buying will occur, and conversely more professional selling. The professional trader profits by taking advantage of the public's reaction to the news, and the amateur pays dearly for waiting for it. In short, the whisper number is a joke. Any whispers I ever hear in life are usually negative and the people doing the whispering I usually don't like any more than the stuff they are saying. Overall, I have the same sentiment when it comes to earnings whispers. As I wrote this, I realized how much I just sounded like Andy Rooney there. Sorry!

To recognize where the pros are putting their money, you need to pay close attention to the price patterns of the stock several days before the company will report.

When a stock is relatively stable in the weeks leading up to an earnings run, you can measure expectation very effectively by the volume and movement in the price of a stock. This will show where the money flow is, bullish or bearish. Find that trend and join it as soon as possible. Do not wait for too much certainty in the trend or you will risk missing the play entirely. This is not the appropriate trade for "scared money." If a stock begins to show high volume and price adjustment in the positive direction, go long. At this point you have a decision to make. Do you want to ride the wave for the next few days for a larger point move? Or do you take many small profits by buying and selling intraday during the time leading up to the actual earnings report? Either way, in this example, your overall sentiment for this stock will tend to be bullish up until the day earnings are reported if the money flow was strong to the buy side.

The first time you use this technique you may have a tendency to try and make the trade work no matter what. But do not find the first company you come across that will report earnings. Choose stocks that have a good earnings history and plenty of daily volume in order to get out fast if you need to. Trying to sell a stock when there isn't anyone buying is no picnic. Put another way, if a thousand people are all heading for the exit door of a burning building at the same time, most will not get out. Yes, this is a harsh example, but trading is real business and if you don't get this straight in your head, especially in terms of liquidity, you will be sorely disappointed. The electronic systems available today will serve you no better than a young person trying to race a Formula One race car with no formal training. In fact, they only accelerate your losses.

To start, trade liquid stocks with a good stable earnings history. Then read a pattern. If a pattern isn't visible to you several days prior to the earnings report, don't trade that stock. Yes, volatility creates trade opportunities, but ignorance creates trade disasters. I often cannot get the rhythm of a stock, and when I can't, I humble myself and walk away, with my cash! New traders often feed the validity to the cliché "Haste makes waste."

The question comes often: Where do I find these earnings calendars, and to which stocks or sectors should I be attracted?

The tech sector of the NASDAQ is always a good place to look for earnings plays. These companies are continuously reinventing themselves to stay on the cutting edge of technology. Because they are growth stocks and competition in this sector is fierce, they offer the volatility and rapid movement to be great candidates for E-DAT.

Technology, in and of itself, is now, in my opinion, the driving force of our economy and the world's economy. It provides the greatest opportunities because it is generating change at a high velocity. Ninety percent of the best-selling products today did not even exist a decade ago, nor do 90 percent of the jobs we'll be doing 10 years from now. The bull market I have traded during my entire career is the product of the innovation, change, and energy spawned by our advancing technological revolution. The evolution from a factory-based/service-based economy to a technology-based economy fuels our stock markets. For this reason, I believe, the fastest-growing and most-liquid markets will be screen-based markets, such as the NASDAQ.

Avoid trading earnings plays with the blue-chip stocks, like Coca-Cola, McDonald's, etc. These corporations pay their dividends to stockholders and invest very little in R&D by comparison to the techies. They trade in a very narrow range over long periods of time. They lack the volatility you want as an E-DAT trader, in terms of rapid, large price movements. Technical analysts would call this trading range *channeling,* which describes the range of motion a stock has from a support and resistance perspective.

You can trade either heavy or light. If you anticipate holding the trade for numerous days, plan on trading light, meaning smaller volume. The longer you are in a trade, the more market risk you expose yourself to, which is compensated for by lowering your volume, to be offset by larger point moves in the stock. This practice of hedging your risk is a common, effective practice worth employing if you plan on a longer-duration trade. As a rule, I do not recommend holding positions over the weekend even if you expect the full course of the earnings play to run for more than a week. Many professionals agree that it's better to exit and then reenter the position. Figure 8-1 shows numerous possibilities for trade entry and exit points.

Electronic day traders should trade heavy. This trade works best the morning after the stock's earnings are announced. Assuming good earnings, the stock tends to gap up considerably, and it experiences some additional positive moves from the buying public on the good news. (Remember, gap openings are when market makers bid the stock higher in order to anticipate demand and bring sellers to the market due to the higher bid price. This in theory is how they help keep an orderly market, because without the additional strength in the bid, sellers theoretically would not come forward.) The stock's price sharply reverses, as the professional money continues selling into the buying public. The reversal is often fast and deep enough to offer an excellent day trade or short-term opportunity to the short side. The day trade is my favorite because there are so many stocks reporting earnings that I can stay busy with those stocks and reduce my market exposure by not carrying positions overnight, and never over a weekend.

Keep in mind, as the reporting day approaches, the whisper number becomes known to almost the entire investment community. The result will be a slower moving and more stable price pattern. This is a very risky stage of the trade and the time to sell into the public buying on favorable news or to buy out the sellers on the expectation of bad news.

It is a good idea to close the position early before the news comes out. Be prepared to take a position on the other side of the market after the event. Professionals often short as the whisper number becomes public, usually the day the report is released. They sell into the liquidity caused by the buy orders of the public, just as the public learns just how good earnings are.

THE SHORT-TERM MOMENTUM TRADE

Another trade ideally suited for the E-DAT trader is the classic short-term momentum trade on the day after the earnings are reported. The key is to expect a reversal off of the morning gap up. Enter your short early enough to get an uptick as the public is still buying, but while the volume is beginning to slow. Be prepared to see a little more heat in this play since the stock will tend to rise further as the public continues to buy, but should roll over due to the overreaction to the earnings news and the market makers' inherent tendency to gap the stocks too high. Once the reversal occurs, your opportunity to buy the stock back at a lower price than your opening short is where your profit is. See Figure 6-1. Of course there is no guarantee that all stocks will react the same way, but the strategy has proved successful for many E-DAT traders who understand trade management.

Even though there are no absolutes in the market or in these earnings plays, keep in mind that the sophisticated traders do not wait to react. Rather, they view how such rumor or news affects the public's expectation. Then they trade the anticipated overreaction. It is a dogfight out there, so once again don't be too literal. If you don't like the way the stock is reacting or what you visualized of the trade is not clear, it is time to cover the trade and move on. The electronic tools available to you today give you the ability to see tick-by-tick, trade-by-trade how the stock is reacting. There is no reason to stay in a trade you no longer understand. Discipline has always been and always will be, in my opinion, the most important attribute the electronic trader, or any trader, can have. Unfortunately, the only electric impulses that can give you discipline are the ones in your brain, so don't forget to use them.

Conditional electronic execution systems are available or will be shortly. I have spoken to a company that is ready to launch a system that will allow the trader to preload the trade parameters into the software, which will automatically exit a position when the criteria are met. For example, if a smart trader knows he or she will only tolerate a half-point loss, that condition can be preloaded into this execution system prior to the trade. Once that parameter is met, the system will automatically send a covering order to close the trade. Even discipline can be written into your trading platform, and that is really exciting, but I personally like to maintain that control myself.

I love earnings because they put a stock in motion. The average investor usually reacts too late, and the motion they anticipate once in the trade is usually the wrong way. But by reading the pattern of the stock ahead of the news, you can read the minds of the professional trading community, and that is where you want to be.

In the next chapter we cover splits. The public seems to have a love affair with this play!

CHAPTER 9

STOCK SPLITS AND RATINGS CHANGES

T he more strategies you learn, the richer you can become. This
chapter offers a few more trading opportunities that can be
used by either the day trader (or E-DAT scalper, as I call him)
or the swing trader who holds positions for a few days.

THE STOCK SPLIT

I think of splits the way I think of IPOs. I also think of two things my
father always said: "All that glitters is not gold," and "You have to die
before you go to heaven." Splits, like IPOs, are rarely the play they
appear to be. In fact, when I see a new trader walk into our office
with one of these stock split beepers, I realize I have a lot of work to
do. My point is that splits are not easy money.

Most people like to play a stock split at the announcement and
this is why some carry those funny beepers (the true definition of
dumb money). The reality is that most splits are announced after
market hours in order to prevent what again has been referred to by
Alan Greenspan, current chairman of the Federal Reserve Board, as

"irrational exuberance." I rarely will buy a stock upon the announcement of a split because of the first reason already mentioned: Splits are announced as a rule after hours. The second reason is because market makers on the NASDAQ gap up the stock to what is usually an artificially high price the first trading day after the split is announced. Also remember that the specialist on the NYSE has the ability to delay the opening of a stock or halt the trading of a listed stock and this power gives the specialist time to sort out all the chaos. This is another reason why the announcement of a split is a dangerous play.

Stock splits have long been the object of desire for traders and investors alike. I believe this is true because first and foremost, a stock split is a bullish event. Meaning, splits simply do not happen, except for a few exceptions, unless the stock is on the move to the upside. The public has, and always will have, a strong appetite for stocks that are moving up, as opposed to stocks that are heading down. We, as traders, need to see the market from both sides. There are opportunities in splits for the E-DAT trader from the short side as well as the long.

Let's first discuss the true purpose of stock splits. They are marketing stunts. Splits create an illusion that stocks are heading up rapidly. As a result of the perception and hype associated with them, they often do go up. Take away the hype and what you really have is a marketing stunt that feeds the public a false illusion of reality. The fact is the stock is worth exactly what it was prior to the split. So why are stock splits declared?

The answer is that the companies want affordable stock for investors. They would much rather have average investors owning their stock than institutional investors, hedge funds, mutual funds, and other professionals. The reason for this is that average investors are much less trouble than institutional money or professional traders. The public believes that the split stock is affordable and will buy it in larger quantities as a split versus the pre-split stock. As a result, the public ends up controlling much of the outstanding shares, reducing the anxiety to the board of directors of that company. The average investor does not ask a lot of questions; institutional investors, such as mutual funds, do. After all, could you imagine an average investor tearing apart the financials of a company before investing the way that a chartered financial analyst of a mutual fund certainly would? Therefore, splits create a perception that stock is affordable to investors who would not have otherwise purchased the stock due to its high cost.

Knowing that stock splits are bullish events and basically marketing stunts, it is also important to note that stock splits tend to have a longer life in terms of the playability of the stock. A split presents a number of different plays. With these facts stated, let us look at the life cycle of splits.

THE POST ANNOUNCEMENT PLAY

A short-term trader (one to three days) can play the stock after the announcement of a split. This trade generally plays out in about one to three days, depending on the volume and recognition of the stock in the public eye. It is important to closely monitor volume and consensus of the stock during the postannouncement period to avoid buying into a selling market, or vice versa.

Here is what you are looking for. Most stocks surge immediately after the split and continue to ascend to a point of overvaluation. This can occur due to the market maker bidding the stock high or low due to the public's overreaction to the news. Whatever the reason the stock reaches a point of overvaluation or how it gets there, the E-DAT should watch for the volume for a sign that it is beginning to subside and look for an opportunity to go short. The discipline needed for this play will never be more important. If the stock begins to run away from you, you need to cover immediately and buy back the borrowed stock. The reason is that while shorting a stock, your risk is theoretically unlimited because stock can go higher and higher to indefinite levels; while going long, stock can only fall to zero. The more realistic reason is that the split occurred because the stock was on the move to the upside, and the company is doing well, represented by its high price, and the reason for the split. So why short a stock in light of all this good news? Because the public will overreact and buy the stock upon the announcement of the split. The people who bought those beepers will definitely use them! Seriously, many will buy the stock upon the announcement, and the stock will probably hit a near 52-week high, if not an all-time high. The history of splits has shown that a sell off will generally occur as the buying volume slows near this 52-week high price.

The reversal that generally takes place after a stock runs up due to the split announcement is referred to as a *retracement*. The stock will generally retrace as much as 10 percent from its high after the announcement. Think of this reversal, or retracement, as a "breather" for the stock. This reversal is a very shortable opportunity, but remember the stock is still going to have upside bias for the longer term. It is only taking a breather.

The upside bias, after this retracement, could once again send the stock to a new high or at least close to it. This presents yet another play to take advantage of before the actual split occurs.

THE POST ANNOUNCEMENT/PRE SPLIT PLAY

You may ask, Why will the stock trade up again? Think of the market makers, hedge funds, and deep-pocket traders as the aristocrats. They have all the money they need and can afford to drive up the price to an overvalued level, in anticipation of selling the stock back to the public after the split, when it is more affordable. Keep in mind these analogies I use are meant with no disrespect, but do accurately describe the sentiment the Street has of the public or dumb money, as they call it. I think this attitude motivates me, as a small trader by comparison, to trade like the aristocrats without the dough. A "beat them at their own game!" The point of this third trade technique is to buy again before the split and sell into the buying public after the pay date when the split occurs. Also remember that buying again here is the price level close to where you covered your short from the "breather." Simply buy to cover your short, and buy again to open your long if you like the way the stock is reacting. Don't be too literal; these entry and exit points are only a guide.

Can you believe the trades you could have—and the stock hasn't even split yet! You've just got to love it!

THE POST SPLIT SPIKE

When the actual split occurs, the things to evaluate are the large gap openings the day after the split, which will take place after the bell. This is where the professional traders want to be careful. Stocks can get out of the zone here a bit, mainly due to the fact that certainty has set in and everyone knows the stock split, which creates another rash of hype. The public begins buying the stock since it is now affordable as noted earlier. This drives the price up once again creating the post split spike.

As a day trader, you can play it two ways, the upside and the reversal, which will occur the same day of the split. As a swing trader (one- to five-day hold), you sell the long position started before the split. What is noteworthy is the stock is still rising and the public is still buying, which gives you enough liquidity to sell. Therefore, be sure to use this opportunity to sell your longs at or near the open the morning after the actual split pay date. Once the public reaction is over, the stock will fall fast, but recover fast also.

Additionally, it is important to look at the angle of attack of the post split spike (refer back to Figures 4-9, 4-10, and 4-11). This means the sharpness of the spike or how quickly the stock trades up. "Irrational exuberance" is often seen at this stage of the split, similar to the announcement stage. See Figure 9-1.

A severe upward trend in the stock indicates the public's strong passion for the stock and is an early warning that the stock will run out of gas quickly. Hence position yourself to sell into the buying public with a reasonable gain.

A medium angle of attack would be classified as levelheaded optimism for the stock in terms of the post split spikes' ascent. Here the stock will take more time to trade up off the split and reverse with less severity as well. Once again, do not take this insight too literally, while staying very cognizant of the fact that stock-split trading is not an exact science.

FIGURE 9-1   *The stock split is all hype and profit. You must be ready to react fast when the news of a split hits the market.*

The Stock Split

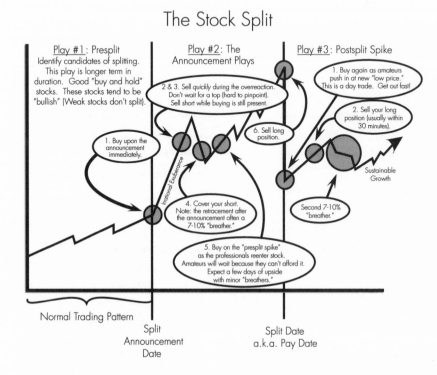

A flatter ascent indicates the stock may continue to grow steadily after the split, similar in path to the stock's normal angle before the stock split. This indicates the stock will trend up again over time and follow similar resistance and support lines, but at the new split-price levels. In other words, a flatter spike indicates that a more sustainable growth pattern is expected and a less severe reversal, if any at all.

The final trade opportunity that exists would be on the second retracement of the stock after the split and spike. This is where the stock reverses or retraces back off the post split spike. Here you could short once again. By this time the stock has lost much of its price elasticity and is pretty much played out in the absence of any new news. It is best to look for new trades in different stocks. Chaos will begin to set in and the plays are more difficult to see in terms of day trading and swing trading. Therefore do not push a bad position or try to make something happen when clarity is elusive.

TRADE THE GRADE

This trade is one of my all-time favorite trades because of its reliability. It is the best reason for getting the best news feed you can afford. I use the Dow-Jones News Service. Earnings reports, product development news, as well as Federal Reserve Board announcements can cause significant movements in stock prices. (And do not forget the NASDAQ stocks when they get added or dropped from an index.) Nothing more quickly and dramatically affects stock prices than upgrades or downgrades by analysts. When you trade up/down grades, you must be aware that the reaction to them is different than it is to earnings announcements.

You know in advance when earnings are due. Based on the consensus estimates of analysts, you have a good idea what to expect. These expectations cause professionals to buy or sell the stock ahead of the earnings announcement. This means the earnings announcements are not a surprise and that they affect prices only if they are substantially different from expectations.

Upgrades and downgrades, on the other hand, are always surprises. They are not announced in advance, but simply indications of a change in sentiment in a given stock by a given firm. They express an opinion of the stock and, as I said before, perception is reality in the market. The reaction to a change in recommendation is often dramatic. Traders will react.

Each firm has its own language to reflect changes in their recommendations. Some examples are:

We recommend this stock to be "accumulated" (upgrade)

We have added this stock to our "recommended list" (upgrade)

This stock has been added to our "buy list" (upgrade)

We have taken this stock off our "buy list" (downgrade)

We recommend a long-term "hold" (downgrade)

Analysts are reluctant to write sell recommendations, which means "hold" is often the closest thing to a sell recommendation you will see.

When the public hears about various market makers (e.g., Goldman Sachs) upgrading or downgrading certain stocks on their recommended lists, the reports usually concern the largest and best-known companies. One hears about these companies simply because they are more newsworthy. What about the less well-known companies that are not likely to be reported on by CNBC, Bloomberg, or the other major financial news networks? The lesser-known stocks make excellent plays as well. As a matter of fact, they are often the best trades because they are purer, meaning less market noise and chaos surround them. They also tend to move more orderly and give you more time to react.

These changes in recommendations are fairly straightforward trading plays because they are not a serious attempt to manipulate public opinions. In order to trade these events, you need to be able to answer the following questions:

- Where can you get a consistent source of this news?
- How do you trade them?
- Which stocks respond the most to this type of news?

Let's first explore when and where to find up/down grades. Almost entirely, the upgrades and downgrades by market-making firms are announced just before the opening. This is important, and in contrast to earnings news, which is almost entirely reported after the close. Many good news sources, like the ones listed below, are available with trading software platforms.

Ratings changes can be found at:

Briefing.com

Zacks.com

Reports from brokerage firms

CNBC

Dow-Jones News Wire, which can be made available to individual traders

The key thing to remember is that reactions to the change in grade are usually overreactions. On upgrades, the public often overbuys the stock out of greed. They remember that another stock acted the same way and someone they knew made a windfall. They are trying to wish something to happen that may not really be there. This is where you may see a gap opening on NASDAQ or a delayed open on a listed stock, as the specialist seeks price equilibrium. It has been said that "amateurs control the open and professionals control the close." Therefore, gaps rarely hold. If a stock gaps open, say four or five points, the astute E-DAT trader fires a sell order into the buying public, anticipating a sharp reversal. This presents a classic shorting opportunity, ideally suited for electronic trading because of the short duration of the move. The market quickly corrects itself from the excessive buying and seeks price equilibrium.

This is like mounting a major media assault announcing "Beanie Babies available!" How would the public react? They overbuy the item and drive the price to an unrealistic level before reality sets in. The parents, who paid $200 for a $20 item, soon come to the conclusion they were caught up in the hype. Price eventually retraces to more realistic levels.

At the NYSE, the specialist has the authority to neutralize the momentum of the public's initial reaction to an upgrade and often delays the opening to accomplish this. The specialist takes what time he or she needs to process and record the orders. It is just that simple. The Wall Street pros rarely get caught up in this type of play. They realize that the dumb money is pouring in, so they sell into the buying public. Then they cover after the stock finds its price equilibrium. This is how the "short off the morning call" is played following gap openings.

This is another good reason for not taking overnight or weekend positions. Gaps happen fast and unexpectedly. Worse, they usually seem to go against you. This is also why market makers announce upgrades or downgrades right before, instead of after, the opening. The news is fresh and allows the specialist some time to process a flood of incoming orders. Plus the market maker is prepared to take advantage of the anticipated move caused by the announcement.

The stocks that respond best to up/downgrades are the listed stocks. Stay away from NASDAQ stocks as a rule. The reason is that listed stocks generally trade in a narrow range, within the support and resistance levels discussed in Chapter 4. More importantly, their movement back to equilibrium is more predictable. You can trade either upgrades and downgrades on bellwether stocks, such as GM, McDonald's, IBM, Disney, or the less well-known listed stocks.

The stronger the message issued by the analyst, the stronger the expected reaction. A strong buy or sell has a huge impact. Other messages, more subtle messages, like an upgrade from a long-term hold to a buy, generate weaker reactions. The more you pay attention to upgrades and downgrades and study the reaction to these events, the more you will be able to recognize if, when, and how to trade the grade.

By now you should be feeling pretty good about the fact that the market moves in mysterious ways, but also in predictable ways. The patterns I have been speaking about and the way in which market professionals respond are exactly the perspective you want to look for while viewing a Level II screen. The E-DAT has a huge advantage over the general public who are not equipped with the tools of technology or knowledge that we have covered thus far. This perspective is the vantage point that will yield you the greatest success when implemented with a dose of common sense, discipline, and patience. Sometimes the best trades are the ones to the short side as the overreaction sets in on good news, or to the long side on overreaction to bad news. Waiting for the overreaction and going the other way can be a high-percentage trading strategy. Patience and a real-time electronic direct access trading system will allow you to see it.

This concludes the section on strategy, but it begins a hugely important section on practicing what you know. The next chapter on simulators will help you to zero in on what systems work best, and why they are important before you put your capital at risk.

Choose a few strategies to start with that we have covered so far and implement them one at a time in a live, active market, but on a simulator with cyber dollars at risk. You will soon feel the exhilaration of gaining confidence, while losing fear, and prepare yourself to enter the market with all the tools you need. The best computer system is the one sitting on your shoulders; no electronic trading system can improve that.

10

THE SIMULATOR

B efore a pilot takes off in a multimillion-dollar aircraft, he gets some serious time in a flight simulator. You need to consider doing the exact same thing. There are stock trading simulators that even utilize live price quotation services. They will give you the opportunity of testing the trading strategies discussed. You get as close an insight as possible into how E-DAT really works, without actually risking your own money. It is an adrenaline rush without the risk. Obviously not 100 percent accurate, but a great transition to trading live.

SELECTING A SIMULATOR

Simulators are available to you over the Internet. They can be run on most home computers with Windows 95 or better, 200 MHz processor, 32 MB RAM, 1.6 GB free hard drive memory, and at least a 56 Kbps modem. Some simulators require access to additional programs, such as Excel. Be sure to check specifications before ordering a simulator service.

The one component you might think about upgrading, once you begin to trade regularly, is your monitor. You might want to go to a large screen (21 inches) with high resolution. The reason is that traders often have as many as 12 windows open at any one time and several of them include charts. Smaller, low-resolution monitors are often difficult to read, especially when you are trading under pressure. Additionally, good programs such as the TradeWise System powered by Real Tick III allow for the Web browser to be active while trading.

Another key area is service. It is important to understand exactly what you must do in the way of setup and how much training is needed. The better simulators can generally be operated intuitively and include the basic trade screen already set up. Additionally, you will want to be comfortable with the level of technical support available to you. The cost of accessing a top-quality simulator runs around $250 to $400 per month, including exchange fees for live price quotations. Never rent a simulator that does not have a live version with which you can actually trade. You should not need the simulator for more than a week or two and many trading schools include it as part of the tuition.

This brings up two questions. First, what is a top-quality simulator and how much practice time do you need? Any simulator I would recommend would include access to live price quotes. This is one of the major input costs of the simulator. Live quotes, as opposed to 15-minute delay, require paying the exchanges a fee. Without real-time quotations, you simply cannot get the true feel of real electronic direct access trading. Using delayed quotes is like taking a shower with a raincoat on—you just do not get the real feel for actual market conditions and trading.

Top-notch simulators are very user friendly. This is key because, when the adrenaline begins to flow, you do not want to have to remember a lot of tricky commands, such as "hold down the Ctrl and the Alt keys while pressing F12." The best systems let you use a mouse and hot keys. For example, let's say you are looking at the screen you normally trade from, the Trade screen. It may have 12 or more windows open. One of the windows is usually the Market Minder screen, which monitors the stocks you are interested in that day. You can see at a glance the symbol, open, net change, percent change, and trend. The other windows show price charts with studies, time and sales, the market makers, and so on.

The stock in the price charts, time and sale, and market maker screens is the active stock at the moment. But what do you do if you notice, or have an alarm set to warn you, that one of the other stocks in your Market Minder screen is making a move? The better-designed simulators allow you to simply drag the symbol of that stock to one of the chart screens and drop it. Other quality systems allow for hot keys, which, with the simple press of a button, will add preloaded stocks to your Level II. Instantly, all your stock-specific screens display data on that stock. You have everything you need to make a decision right in front of you.

If you have certain technical analytic studies, like specific oscillators or stochastic tools, you use regularly, you might want to check to see if they are available on the simulator. Most packages provide all the common analytic tools. You must also be able to customize the charts of the stocks you trade. For example, you might want to see daily, 5-day, and 30-day charts simultaneously. Then you can overlay trend lines, moving averages, oscillators, or analytic tools on the charts.

There is a big difference between a simulator and demonstration-only software—do not be fooled. You want to be sure you are using a program that simulates live trading. To be sure, ask what price-quote package is tied into the trading software package. Quality systems tie your quotes to real-time quotes.

Once you spot a trade from the trade screen, the normal procedure is to hit a function key to call up the Trade Entry or Execution screen. This screen embodies all the power of electronic trading. You can now access NASDAQ market makers and NYSE specialists directly—at the speed of light. You are now "hot." Most simulators allow you to make mock trades with cyber dollars. These trades look and feel like the real thing, but are not actually sent to the exchanges. A subprogram looks at the current market and matches your order with the market if your price is within trading range. Although simulating true market liquidity is difficult, I have seen some systems that are 70% accurate in my opinion, which is pretty good.

Remember the simulator should be an exact mirror of the real trading program. When your orders are filled, they change color on most systems. There may also be a separate trade monitor window that tells you what you traded, when, and if you are "in the money, at the money, or out of the money." Some even include a dynamic profit-and-loss ledger. For example, you place an order to buy 1000 shares of XON (Exxon). It is a long buy that might show up on the screen in green. Open orders are red. If you shorted a stock, the original color might be magenta or purple. When filled, it could change to yellow and then to green when covered. A canceled order might also show up black. The colors can vary by system, but it is important that the software you select have a very simple system like this. You must be able to glance at your order-entry screen and be able to tell immediately what orders are open, canceled, filled, or still working.

ACTUAL TRADING

In most cases, all orders submitted electronically are considered day orders and are canceled at the end of the trading session or sooner in the case of SelectNet. But never make assumptions when it comes to orders. Have your broker-dealer supply you with the exact handling procedures. If an exchange cancels your order at the end of the session, what happens at the ECN? Some cancel orders when the exchanges close and others keep your orders working until they shut down. This means, you could be filled by a match on an ECN, after the NASDAQ closes. If you get a decent fill, that is okay. But what if you get filled unexpectedly and do not want it? You own it anyway. All the better systems tell you if any orders are not filled, so you know your order is still working.

To enter an order, you input the symbol for the stock in the proper box in the order-execution window. If it is a market order, you designate it as such. It there is a price limit on your order, you input this and the limit price. Naturally you must show volume in number of shares. Some systems, like SOES, require that you accept partial fills.

After that, you must select the routing. Do you go SOES, Select-Net, SuperDot or one of the ECNs? The trading software programs are not set up to trade through every possible system. The reasons are threefold. First, each ECN requires a different software subroutine to allow the various trading software programs to access it. If the trading software does not have that subroutine, it cannot connect with the ECN. Most of the trading programs access the key trading networks, such as SOES, SuperDot, SelectNet, and several ECNs. For example, they might link up with ISLD (Island) and BTRD (Bloomberg), but not provide access to TNTO (Archipelago) or REDI (RediBook).

The second reason for not providing access to every possible route is cost. There is usually a fee associated with accessing and getting setup on an ECN. Last of all, there is some redundancy within the ECNs. Several of the ECN services overlay, and there is no need to subscribe to every one of them. The best trading environment offers an integrated trading platform to allow the trader to decide which ECN to use and how to trade the order. All ECNs live and die by the size of their order flow, which is liquidity. Without liquidity, they cannot fill trades and that is where they make their money. I suggest trading on ECNs that will provide the most liquidity. For example, if your order is sent to an ECN but is not filled, will that ECN send your order elsewhere to complete it? The best systems will.

My point is that you must have a pretty good idea of what routes you will be using to get your orders filled and select your trading software based on those needs. Also I would recommend you always try to get a system that includes Island. Having Island is important because it gives you access to the Island book of orders at all times. Being able to see the Island book helps you see where the other traders are, which we discussed in Chapter 5. InstiNet has the most liquidity, but it is hard to get access to, and only the top electronic brokerage firms can get you on it, but only if you trade in house at their office. As you shop around for systems, the key to a good ECN is liquidity.

CONSIDERATIONS AND RULES

The material that follows may or may not apply to every trading software package on the market. But it applies to most. I include it to prepare you, so you have a feel for how the programs are written. You must take the time and spend the money to learn thoroughly whatever software you choose. That's why I stress the value of working on a simulator before trading in real time.

For example, on some systems if you double-click the Island ECN to buy 1000 shares of a stock, you could very well own 2000 instead. If you've gotten into the bad habit of double clicking on every box, you could have problems with some of the software programs. Two clicks often send two orders. Another common error is attempting to use a SOES order on an ECN. You would get an error message canceling your order, and it could mean a sweet opportunity missed. Good broker-dealers will offer schools not just for the software but for trading techniques as well. That is why I prefer an E-DAT broker-dealer with a branch office system. On-line trading systems are available, but you seem to be on your own without a place to go to when you need help. If the broker-dealer you trade with has an office, trading floor, and school, you can always go back to the branch to get your batteries recharged.

Here is another example. Let's say you have a SOES order priced at the inside market. But before it is completed ISLD (Island, an ECN) moves to the top of the inside market. Your pending SOES execution gets canceled, since you cannot SOES an ECN. This illustrates an important distinction between ECNs and SOES. If you SOES a market maker, the market maker must fill your order, if you are the first to hit it. The market maker cannot back away from the order, but the order must be within the inside market. You use an ECN to show the market your intentions, or at what price you are willing to buy or sell a stock. That price can be outside the market, which means it is higher than the current offer or below the current bid. If a market maker or some other E-DAT trader likes what you present to the market, they will take you up on it and execute against your order. The point is, E-DAT offers a huge advantage over on-line trading, but because it is more sophisticated it requires some education.

Another error to avoid is selling short on a downtick. Your broker is forced to buy you in to cover the short, which is the same as buying a losing trade. Good software will prevent you from doing this. I recommend you try it when trading on a simulator to see how the software handles trading-rule violations. Another way to waste valuable execution time is putting an offer on SelectNet at a price outside the spread. Your order will be canceled. All your offers to buy or to sell must be within the spread or inside market, except when using ECNs.

You must be aware that SOES has a 15-second and a 2-hit rule for the market maker. Market makers can be hit on the bid or ask only twice at the same price and they may wait 15 seconds between those two hits before taking the second order. After they have been hit two times, they can refresh the bid and ask or withdraw it and adjust their price. If your SOES orders are not taken, this is probably the reason. Therefore don't chase the stock. Try the order on Select-Net or reenter the order. Also, stay away from limit orders during a high-velocity trade. Use market orders, because with E-DAT systems, there is less slippage. This is especially true when compared to an on-line trading system that will sell your order to a broker's broker or stock wholesaler.

Canceling orders takes some care on electronic systems. Clicking the cancel button on an active order usually handles it on most systems. Your order is live until your system confirms it is killed. If you press cancel, but your order is executed before the order is killed and confirmed on SOES, SelectNet, or SuperDot, you own the trade.

SOME GOOD HABITS TO LEARN

The best habit you can get into is proofreading each order-entry screen twice before clicking the execute button. Personally, I read the order from front to back and then back to front. The speed of execution keeps me from becoming sloppy.

While you are still trading on a simulator, practice changing prices in the price window to unusual numbers, such as ½₂, prior to actually needing them. Some software allows you to scroll between fractions, which is a good tool. Another good thing to practice is changing the order from buy to sell. On some systems you can right click the mouse as a short cut to the sell command. This comes in handy when you want to buy on the bid or sell on the offer. A common error, on these systems, is to inadvertently click and execute trades on the wrong side and consequently overbuy or oversell. The best systems allow you to let the system activate a trade confirmation before it sends the order, similar to a safety on a gun. As you get better, you can disable the feature.

TIPS ON ROUTING ORDERS

Prices for limit orders must be set to the inside bids or asks (offers) or the system immediately cancels the orders on SOES or SelectNet. You can trade outside the market on ECNs. For example, you see a stock retracing, but you also believe it will hit a support level and recover. You can use an ECN to put a buy order below the current bid and wait for the stock to come to you. If the stock begins to fall faster than expected and you decide to cancel your order to see where the stock actually does find support, you can do that instantly on an E-DAT system. These are advantages you don't have with traditional on-line brokerage accounts.

Some slippage is possible in the SOES system due to its priority structure. SOES orders are processed on a first-come, first-served basis. Similar orders are placed in a queue for execution. By using limit orders and missing the trades, you continually lose your place in line each time you have to reenter orders. You must use market orders when you really want to make that trade.

SelectNet orders may be executed by market makers in any order they want. Remember that it is a nonmandatory system. With SelectNet a market maker can take any offer it wants, regardless of priority. Your bid or offer is guaranteed for three minutes, but it is not uncommon for it to last longer. On SelectNet, only the market maker sees the orders. You have a limited audience. You may send your order only to a single market maker with which you wish to trade, using the Preference function. This is available on SelectNet only. Remember that SelectNet orders are not represented on the Level II screen.

As ECN's such as Archipelago come on-line, the need for SelectNet diminishes, since these ECNs will automatically find you the liquidity to get in and out of trades—and this is very powerful.

TRADING TERMINOLOGY

The following is some terminology you may run into as you begin to trade electronically, especially if you have an experienced trader helping you or you are attending a school or seminar. You may find it useful to have a handle on the jargon.

"Hitting the bid" means selling at the bid price.

"Lifting the offer" means buying at the offered price.

"Working" means the order is still live.

"Out" means cancel the order.

"Cancel" means cancel the order.

"Not held" means an order submitted to a broker does not necessarily have to be filled and the broker is not liable.

"Go down to" means that if the trader is working an offer at 79 and wishes to revise and sell at 78¾, the trader says, "Go down to 78¾."

"Pay up to" means the exact opposite of "Go down to." If a trader is working an order at 49 and wants to revise and buy at 49½, the trader says, "Pay up to 49½."

"Handle" means the nonfractional part of a price. For example in 110¾, the 110 is the handle. The handle is also sometimes referred to as "the figure."

"Shave" means to reduce the quantity.

This language is also important because many E-DAT firms will allow you to call their trading desk and place orders. If you have technical difficulty or just want to speak to a broker, top-notch firms will have a toll-free number to call the trading desk. Knowing how to speak will save you time and help assure you are understood.

E-DAT requires careful attention to detail. There are no short-cuts to success. I simply cannot stress enough how the time spent practicing the strategies and the special rules on a simulator can pay off when you actually begin to trade.

In Chapter 11, I will help you find a quality broker-dealer to start your E-DAT account with addressing key issues you should know before you send in your money.

11

OPENING AN
E-DAT ACCOUNT

There are no special regulations from the Securities Exchange Commission, the National Association of Securities Dealers, or the New York Stock Exchange pertaining specifically to individual electronic traders—yet. It is hard to imagine that there will not be some changes at some time in the future. For now, opening an account to trade electronically is basically the same as opening a traditional trading account. You get access to the same trading tools the professionals have without having to be licensed. You have the benefits, sans the regulation and oversight bureaucracy. The only difference I have seen is that most broker-dealers, or stock brokerage offices, that can handle this specialty ask for some additional disclosure from their customers.

In the securities industry the word *disclosure* means "a warning." When you sign the account papers to open an account, you must agree to all the traditional disclosure statements plus one additional one. Remember, attorneys bought and paid for by broker-dealers with whom you are opening an account write the account papers. They are documents to protect broker-dealers, so be sure to them closely. That does not mean you do not have an advocate. I discuss your advocates later in the chapter.

The protection the broker-dealer seeks, in my opinion, is reasonable. Mostly they ask you to attest in writing that you understand all the fees and regulations involved and that you absolve them of any unusual risks, such as a loss you might incur due to an act of God, such as an exchange computer system crashing from a lightning strike. They are also required by federal regulations to find out enough information from you to determine if you are suitable for the investment strategies that you plan to conduct. To do that they must obtain the following information:

Your true name and actual street address (a Post Office box is not acceptable)

Your principal occupation

Your current estimated annual income, liquid net worth, and total net worth

Your age

Your citizenship

Your previous investing experience

Your investment objectives, which should be short-term for electronic traders

Your marital status and number of dependents

Your social security or tax identification number

The rationale for this information is simple. They need to know where you live and if you are suitable for trading. You can have your statements sent to another address, such a your office or a drop box if you wish. Your occupation helps the manager at the brokerage firm, who must approve all accounts, get a feel for your life experiences and education and compare this to the type of trading you plan to conduct. Plus, knowing the name and nature of your employment tells the broker if you are registered in any capacity with another brokerage firm, which triggers additional regulations.

Your financial situation and ability to meet payment schedules are important. Can you stand behind your trading strategy? The account papers are a legal agreement between you and the broker-dealer; therefore, you must be of legal age in the state in which you open the account. By knowing your citizenship, the broker-dealer knows if you need to sign a W-2 form for tax purposes or a nonresident alien form. Naturally, your previous trading experience and investment objectives are important in determining if you are prepared for the type of trading you plan to do. Knowing about your family obligations helps your broker advise you regarding the types of investments that are best suited for you.

Does this mean, if you just turned 21 with limited assets, you could not open an account? No, the answers to these questions determine what type of account you are eligible for and what type of trading the firm can allow you to do. For example, if you are 21 and undercapitalized, you could open a cash account. This simply means any stocks you buy must be paid for in cash before they are transferred to your name. A margin account, where you were asking the brokerage firm to finance up to half of your purchases, would not be approved until you accumulate some net worth and establish credit lines.

The types of trading strategies you wish to employ are a critical part of the decision regarding what type of account you can open. Margin accounts, governed by the Federal Reserve Board's Regulation T, allow the broker to sell you stocks and finance 50 percent of the purchase. As a way of discouraging or encouraging trading, the Federal Reserve Board can adjust the percentage figure up or down at any time.

Another area, which often puzzles traders, is the various levels of risk involved with options trading strategies. Here are the four basic options strategies in order of risk, lowest to highest:

- *Selling covered calls.* You sell a call on a stock that you own. This strategy is the only option strategy allowed in an Individual Retirement Account (IRA).
- *Buying calls or puts.* A call gives you the option, but not the obligation, to assume a long position in a stock at a given

price for a specific period of time. A put does the same on
the short side.

- *Multiple option strategies.* You buy and sell combinations of
options—spreads, straddles, etc.
- *Selling naked options.* With these, the risk of selling a call is
theoretically unlimited and the risk of selling a put is that the
stock can go to zero. Naked means you do not own the
underlying security on which the option is sold.

When you apply to a brokerage firm to trade options, it will
consider all the information requested earlier (i.e., your financial status, past experience, etc.) and assign the level of options trading it
will permit. Do you have the financial strength to sell a naked call?
Do you have the experience to put on a butterfly spread? The supervisor of new options accounts must make these decisions.

Electronic trading is lightning fast and therefore quality firms
have certain restrictions built right into the software. For example,
suppose you accidentally tried to purchase more stock than you
could afford to pay for. Traditionally, with working through a broker,
the broker would check your account first to see if you had the
assets to make the purchase. With E-DAT, some firms do not have
such restrictions built into the software to stop such an oversight or
mistake. I strongly suggest staying away from such firms.

The possible mistakes and problems are numerous. By the time
a back office supervisor of a firm sees a problem with an account, it
will already have happened. This is again why quality firm selection
is so important.

At present, most broker-dealers accepting electronic trading
accounts require a special agreement alerting their customers to the
unique risks they face. For example, if they are day trading at home
and they lose electrical power, they have a special problem. Most
brokers tell these customers to call into the office and have their
broker take them flat. But any losses belong to the trader, not the
brokerage firm. This includes any errors. For example, the trader
gets hit on an open order after power is lost and does not know
about it and, therefore, does not offset the position. When power is
restored, the position is down $5 per share on a 1000-share lot. That

debit belongs to the trader. For this reason, it is common for electronic traders to include a backup power supply as part of their computer equipment.

Another issue that will arise is the Internet. There are issues that need to be addressed when trading your account over it.

The Internet service provider (ISP) you choose, the telephone connection you have, the need for a second line, technical support, and broker availability and support, are all key concerns to ask about when setting up an E-DAT account, especially over the Internet. I strongly suggest choosing a firm that has alternative means of execution for the traders of the firm for those times when the Internet drops them or when other technical problems arise. Quality firms will have dedicated telephone lines with brokers standing ready to take your calls and alternative means of execution to get you out of trades when these problems occur.

I strongly suggest that you also have a second telephone line to make phone calls when needed. Do not attempt to trade on the same line that you use for the phone. You need a line that is available at all times to call the firm that handles your account. If you cannot call your firm without getting a voice mail system, I suggest choosing a firm that does offer personal broker assistance.

Computer security is another key issue for investors trading at some place where someone other than they might have access to their computer. Let's say a self-employed person trades from his or her office. That person leaves the trading program up when called away for whatever reason. An employee, maliciously or in jest, executes a few trades. Who is responsible? The trading tickets show up at the broker-dealer's office, but there is no way for the dealer to know they are bogus trades. Naturally, the trader is held accountable. It is just another risk the trader assumes and needs to be aware of.

Careful thought must also go into the type of account opened. There are four basic types:

- Individual—one person's name is on the account and that person is solely responsible
- Joint—most commonly a husband and wife, with ownership going to the survivor in the event of death

- Corporate—opened in the name of a corporation with one or more individuals designated to trade the account
- Partnership—more than one person opens the account and all partners are liable for the entire activity of the account and all can trade it

My recommendation for electronic trading is to only open individual accounts. Whenever there is more than one person involved, there is more risk. If you unfortunately die while the account is open, your registered representative (broker) is required to immediately cancel all pending and outstanding transactions. With the other types of accounts, where there can be more than one person placing orders or more than one person accessing the trading software, the possibility of unwanted liabilities grows dramatically. There are trading authorization forms that can be used if more than one person owns the account. For example, a partnership account can authorize only one of the partners as the trader.

When you open an account, besides deciding on type of ownership (individual, joint, corporate, partnership), you must also specify trading authorization. Again, you have four basic choices:

- No discretion—you reserve the right to make each and every trading decision. This is the most common for electronic trading.
- Discretion—you give someone, other than yourself, the power to trade your account, as if it is his or her own. This can be limited to only trading or it can be unlimited discretion, which would include withdrawal of funds. I suggest never giving anyone discretion.
- Fiduciary—the person given the fiduciary responsibility trades the account. This authority is usually reserved for trust accounts, but not suggested for E-DAT and day trading.
- Custodial—the custodian for the beneficial owner (usually a minor) enters all trades.

The first option is self-explanatory. You trade your own account and this is the way most electronic accounts are handled. Some

investors might want to consider the second. The investors give trading authority to their E-DAT brokers, for example, via a limited
power of attorney. The professional trader enters all orders without
having to consult the investor, but I discourage this very much.
Remember, E-DAT is for people who want control. Why incur the
risk of a broker trading your account in a manner you may regret.

A variation of this approach is called a *guided account*. The
client and the broker discuss each trade and develop a definite plan
of action, i.e., the broker is to buy a certain number of shares of a
specific stock when and if certain conditions are met, such as price
or time. The investor instructs the broker to "Buy 1000 shares of
CSCO (Cisco Systems Inc.) when it hits 96. Sell at your discretion
when there is a profit of one-quarter point or more or when it drops
one-quarter." With this type of discretion, no power of attorney is
necessary, but the broker cannot act without definite instructions.
This system works well for investors who like the risk-control aspects
of E-DAT, but lack the time required to keep track of a trade throughout the day.

The other two types of trading authorizations, fiduciary and custodial, might lend themselves to electronic trading, depending on the
specific circumstances and risk factors defining the account. Before
accepting this responsibility, a legal review would be in order.

In the beginning of this chapter, I mentioned that you had an
advocate to protect your rights when dealing with brokers. Your
advocates are the various local, state, and federal agencies that regu-
late the securities industries. Even the United States Postal Service
can help in the case of mail fraud, which can be loosely defined to
cover the account statement sent by your broker. In other words,
your interest as an investor is extremely well protected.

Local regulatory agencies vary by state. If your state does not
have a separate securities regulatory division, you will probably find
such regulation under the secretary of state's jurisdiction. Another
place to go for help if you feel anything illegal has taken place is
your local district attorney.

On the national level, the Congress via the Securities Exchange
Acts of 1933 and 1934 provided for the following:

- Creation of the Securities and Exchange Commission
- Regulation of the exchanges
- Regulation of credit (margin) by the Federal Reserve Board
- Registration of broker-dealers
- Registration of insider transactions, short sales, and proxies
- Regulation of trading activities
- Regulation of client accounts
- Customer protection rules
- Regulation of the over-the-counter markets
- Enforcement of net capital rule

That is a lot of regulating to do, so the Securities and Exchange Commission created some self-regulatory organizations (SRO) to assist. The exchanges, such as the New York Stock Exchange, have their own SRO. It also regulates all broker-dealers who are members of the NYSE.

The National Association of Securities Dealers regulates the over-the-counter markets. The NASD regulates virtually all broker-dealers who electronic traders come in contact with, since the NAS-DAQ is such a big part of electronic trading.

There are two functions of the NASD that can impact you directly. First, the NASD conducts compliance audits of broker-dealers. These audits verify your broker-dealer is following all the regulations. For example, the auditors might check your account papers to see that all the information is complete. If, for example, you did not want to reveal your net worth, the auditors will check to see whether the broker had proof of some other sort that you are suitable for a particular account. You could have submitted a letter to your broker stating your objection, including a statement that, although you refused to state your exact net worth, it exceeds $500,000, which is above the broker-dealer's minimum suitability requirement. If you had refused to provide any information, the broker-dealer should have refused to open your account, which is its right.

The other key function is the investigation of customer complaints. If you have a complaint with a broker or his or her firm that you cannot resolve, my advice is first go to the manager or owner of the firm. Every firm has a vested interest in resolving customer complaints as fast as possible. It is just good business for everyone to cooperate and solve any misunderstandings. It has been my experience that the management of any good firm is more than willing to work out any problem that arises to the customer's satisfaction. If a complaint has merit, a credible broker-dealer will resolve it fairly.

You may be wondering what are some solid grounds for filing a complaint. Losing money in the market? Following bad advice? Following tips that did not pan out? Unfortunately, none of the above. These are all par for the course. You must expect to lose in trading. It is hoped that you will make more than you lose, but no one should give you a guarantee. If someone does, have them put the guarantee in writing, and you will have the grounds for a complaint if you do lose. Bad advice simply means someone does not have the ability to foretell the future. No one does and you cannot blame someone for not having that ability.

On the other hand, here are a few areas in which you could have a complaint:

- If you were high-pressured into opening an account or into conducting a certain trade
- If unreasonable promises were made to you, such as, "You cannot lose trading electronically"
- If you received any fraudulent or deceitful communications from your broker
- If there is unauthorized trading in your account
- If you have given discretion to your broker and excess takes place
- If there are uncorrected errors in your trading account

With the first three, the broker is being untruthful. But in many cases, it is your word against his or hers. Whenever you feel something is not quite right, ask for confirmation in writing. In most cases, the dishonest broker will not provide anything in writing. Therefore, you know it is not true. If you do get something on paper, at least you have some proof.

The last three can be avoided by closely reviewing your statements. Always check them closely. Are the commissions right? Do the trades shown agree with your trading log? Are the prices the same as you recorded? Have all the positions been closed out? Is the math correct? And never hesitate to call your broker with any questions. The broker's primary responsibility is to satisfy your trading needs.

If the broker-dealer or firm wants to stay in business, they will exceed your expectations and not fall short. This has always been my responsibility, morally and from a regulatory perspective, and most other broker-dealers, in my opinion, feel the same way.

In the final chapter I will help you ask yourself the right questions about your trading plan, setting goals, controlling losses, and treating trading like a business.

12

THE VIRTUAL UNIVERSE OF E-DAT

J ust as you would expect new pilots to get some last words of advice from their flight instructor, I would like to share with you some of what I learned from my years of trading. For openers, you need a solid flight plan describing how you are going to trade and manage your money. Then you must select the best brokerage firm available and a mentor. Finally, I will share some advice that I hope will help you avert some of the errors my clients and I have made over the years.

I strongly recommend you develop a trading plan—and put that plan on paper! A written plan does two important things for you. It forces you to make concrete decisions. And it provides you with something you can use to measure your progress, and more importantly, your discipline. How can you "Inspect" what you "Expect" without tracking results?

It's sad for me to recall the number of traders I've seen over the years who have waffled from one approach to another without any clearly stated plan. They wander in and out of the market, often making the same mistakes over and over. If you were to start a business, your banker would demand a written plan. I wish, as a broker-dealer, I could require everyone who opens a trading account with my firm to produce a trading plan. Your written plan need not be fancy. It's not a formal proposal. It could be as simple as answers to the questions asked later in this chapter. But it will help you focus on what you are going to do, how you are going to do it, what you need from outside sources, and what you expect to gain. Lastly, your plan must be flexible. Just because it is on paper does not mean it cannot be completely revised.

WRITING YOUR TRADING PLAN

Step one is describing your trading philosophy and general goals. This can be done in one or two sentences. Here are a few examples.

Example 1
"I plan to be an E-scalper, trading very short-term positions for only a few minutes. My primary strategy will be momentum trading. I will look for trades among the most actively traded NASDAQ stocks in the technology sector."

Example 2
"I'm an electronic day trader. I seek opportunities wherever I can find them. I'll hold trades as long as I have to in order to reach my objective, but not overnight."

Example 3
"My approach is to trade only Intel. I'll concentrate all my energy on that one stock. I'll learn all there is to know about that company, its market makers, and how the stock performs in every type of market."

Example 4
"I plan to continue to be a long-term trader. I'll buy stocks and hold them as long as I still have confidence in their products, management, and future. Electronic trading gives me the ability to enter the market at the most opportune price and exit ahead of trouble if it appears on the horizon."

Example 5
"I'm going to be a swing trader, holding positions for a few days but never over a weekend. I'll shepherd the six stocks I've

been trading for the last few years, and use technical analysis as my decision support tools."

By jotting down your general approach to the market, you set the tone for the rest of the plan. It helps you answer the questions to come.

What are your goals?

We all want to make the most money we can. If we didn't, we'd be buying certificates of deposits or Treasury bonds. Your goals dictate your strategies and must reflect your philosophy. A goal of 50% or 100% return to equity per annum requires a different strategy than a goal of 20% to 30% per year. If these return objectives seem high to you, compared to other types of investments, remember electronic trading is very intense—high volume combined with long hours of research and trading. No pain; no gain. At the same time, E-DAT is risky business, and you can lose your money, so risk management needs to be part of your goals and strategy.

Another good way to set your goal is net profit per day or per week. It could be $100 or $500 per day. If you trade 200 days per year, that adds up to $20,000 to $100,000 per year. Are you going to trade part-time to supplement your current income or full-time? For example, I see clients who work in the afternoons and evening. They trade for three or four hours each morning with the objective of clearing $50 or $100 per day after trading expenses and commissions. Some are housewives who trade after taking their children to school or men who work a swing shift and have their mornings free. On the other extreme are the dedicated full-time traders with their eyes on the trading screen from the opening to the closing bell. Their goals are much more ambitious. Others have weaned in slowly, starting as part-timers and graduating to full-time trading machines.

You can set your goal in terms of trades per day or week and not worry about profitability. This takes some of the pressure off for some traders. It's like a ball player concentrating on hits per game with the idea that the homers will come, if his batting average is high enough. You might set your initial goal at 20 trades per week, with the expectation of at least half closing at a profit. This is often a good way to start.

Let's talk about matching investment goals with strategies. If your return objective is on the conservative side, say you want to supplement your gross income by picking up an extra $2500 per month or $30,000 per year. What must your goal be? Using 20 trading days per month, you would need to net $125 per day. The key here is income, net of expensives. To do this, you need an estimate on expenses.

If you leased everything, your fixed cost might look like this on a monthly basis:

Computer	$ 50
Software (includes trading software and live price quotes)	250
Total	$300

This is assuming you are working out of your home and not charging yourself any rent. Additionally, you would have your variable cost of commissions. Let's call them $25 in and $25 out, or $50 per round turn. If you averaged a quarter of one point profit per successful trade and your batting average is .500, or half your trades are profitable, how many trades would you have to do per day to generate $125 net profit?

A quarter point profit on a 1000-lot trade is $250. Your fixed cost is $15 per day ($300/20 trading days a month). If you made four trades a day and two lost a teenie and the other two made a quarter point, your net would look like this:

Profitable trades gross	$500
Less losing trades	125
Less fixed costs	15
Less miscellaneous costs (second phone line, Internet service, etc.)	25
Less two round-turn commissions	100
Income before taxes	$235

You are at your daily goal. If you rented office space, your overhead would be higher. It is common for the broker-dealer to absorb the cost of your software, if you execute a certain number of trades each day or month. That would reduce your cost by $300 per month. You could lease a seat at a brokerage firm that has trading rooms completely equipped for serious traders. All the services needed—computers, software, news, technical/fundamental information, etc.—are available, including training and coaching by professional traders. Many traders prefer this professional atmosphere to working alone at home or at an office.

My point is that you must decide on a goal and then work out the math to see exactly how realistic it is. The above goal of generating $125 per day is modest, in my estimation, and very attainable. On the other hand, I have met new traders who expected way too much. Your goal must be tempered with your commitment. Is your desire to be a successful electronic trader high, medium, or low? Are you going after this with a passion or just to bring in a few extra bucks? You must make the decision. How will you deal with losses, is another question.

Your goal also depends on your current financial situation. Can you afford to trade full-time or must you continue to work? How much capital can you devote to this project? Do you think you need to attend a seminar or school on electronic trading? These can cost from one to several thousands of dollars and require a full week of your time or a full weekend at the least. You might have to travel to the school and live in a motel for the week. This can bring the cost to over $5,000.

Then there is the initial investment. Opening an account requires from $5,000 to $100,000, depending on the broker-dealer's minimum equity requirement. If you plan to trade full-time, you should have enough money to cover living expenses for six months and a little extra for losses incurred in the beginning. Don't forget that time spent on a good simulator can reduce these costs or convince you to change your style altogether.

This line of thought brings us to the subject of risk. When attempting to measure or quantify risk, economists use the term *util-*

ity, which is a measure of personal satisfaction. If something generates a feeling of greater satisfaction than whatever it is compared to, it is said to have greater utility.

You need to seriously think about how much risk you are psychologically prepared to accept. Do you classify yourself as adverse to risk, as neutral, or as an aggressive risk taker? For example, a risk-adverse person, within the context of electronic trading, may not be interested in a trade that projects a dollar return for every dollar at risk. These traders want to take less risk and are comfortable with low, but dependable, rewards. The electronic day trading and E-DAT scalping strategies appeal to them. The neutral and aggressive risk takers are willing to take greater and greater risks to get higher and higher utility. For electronic traders, that means holding positions for one or more days, for larger point moves.

Think of the stock market as a nuclear reactor—the more you are exposed to radiation the greater the chance of getting burned. Market risk is measured by the amount of time you are in the market. It could be seconds, minutes, hours, days, or weeks. The longer you are in the market the greater the chance something will go wrong. Therefore, the trading style that keeps you in the longest can also be the most risky.

Your personal financial situation and responsibility must also be considered. A single person with a handsome six-figure income can afford to take some risks. On the other hand, the breadwinner of a large family in a middle-income tax bracket should be more conservative.

After sorting through all these thoughts, it's time to write down specific goals that you will shoot for:

Net income of $500 per day or week

10 winning trades per day or per week

A .500 batting average

Set the amount and term to match your strategy. Long-term traders evaluate themselves on a weekly basis. Short-term investors need to think in terms of daily performance. At this point, you are setting targets. You can revise these marks higher or lower the longer you trade. Within a month or two, you should have a really good feel for what you and your trading system can do.

Which markets suit you? The volatile NASDAQ, the more calm NYSE, or either one, depending on where the opportunities are at the time? Write down your choice. Think about how you are going to select trades. What methods? Will you use technical analysis? If so, describe what you plan to do. How are you going to enter and exit trades? How will you set profit goals? Remember that it's possible to get rich by exiting trades "too soon." What is your loss limit going to be? If a trade goes against you a teenie or an eighth, will you cut your losses promptly? If you do not have all these parameters set in advance, you will not be able to make the split-second decisions necessary to trade successfully.

THE TRADE JOURNAL AND DATABASE ANALYSIS

Also consider keeping a trading journal, at least for the first six months or a year. In it include the date, time you began and stopped trading, all your trades by time entered and exited, reason for entering each one, what prompted you to exit, the results, and anything you would do differently next time. Your trading diary does not have to be fancy or even neat. But it does have to give you enough information to compare what you are doing with what you said you were going to do in your plan. If they do not match up, one or the other needs some adjusting. All you are trying to accomplish with the journal is isolate and correct bad habits and replicate successes. This is an outstanding tool to use, particularly if you have a mentor or coach to review it with you.

An advanced version of the trade journal is the trading analysis database. In a relational database, such as Microsoft Access, you list all the important variables. You want to do it in a database so you can query that database looking for patterns in your trading. If you can find your most successful patterns, you can replicate them. Conversely, you want to eliminate your least successful patterns.

Therefore, you need to make a list of the variables for each trade. Some of the most important ones are:

- *Duration of each trade.* Capture the entry and exit time. If you use military time, a 24-hour clock, it is easy for your computer to calculate the duration.
- *Type of trade.* Was it a momentum trade, news-driven, special strategy, such as the earnings play, etc. Give each type you commonly use a code.
- *Day of the week.*
- *Outcome.* Use a simple coding system (s = successful; vs = very successful; l = minor loss; ml = major loss; be = break even; etc.).
- *Profit and loss in whole dollars.*
- *Discipline.* Every trade should have an entry and exit strategy. Did you honestly follow your plan for that trade or did you hope or wish for something good to happen? Just use a simple yes or no. From the chapters on trading, you should by now know the time horizons and other characteristics for each type of trade, which often answers the question of whether you followed or ignored the discipline associated with each type of trade. A violation of discipline, for example, would be to trade heavy when the type of trade called for a light position.
- *Type of execution.* Here you would put SOES, SelectNet, Archipelago, SuperDot, Island, InstiNet, called order into broker, etc.
- *Type of Order.* Limit, market, etc.
- *Sector traded.* Tech, medical, retail, banking, oil, etc.
- *Type of stock traded.* Listed or NASDAQ.
- *Type of analysis.* Don't just put technical versus fundamental. Be more specific, such as TA/support-resistance lines, Level II momentum, shadowing the ax, etc.
- *Long or short sale.*

Once you have a sufficient amount of data inputted into your database, you can use electronic analysis to uncover patterns in your trading. Sufficient data is a function of your level of trading, depending on whether you do 100 trades a day or 100 a month. After 1000 trades you should be able to see some patterns.

The first thing to do is pull a query of all your trades in descending order of profitability. Your most profitable trade to your least profitable. Start to look for patterns. What percentage of the top 10 percent of your trades came from the same market, listed versus NASDAQ? What was the average length of duration? What sectors turned up most often? You can run additional queries to analyze your performance using specific strategies or specific time horizons.

I will venture to guess you will find you do better trading one sector compared to another. That is usually explained by your personal interest in that sector. Or one time horizon may be better per your attention span. Or one type of strategy that you like or have more faith in works best most often. Or a certain type of technical analysis is most satisfying. If you can find out early on what the keys to your success are, you'll be a very happy and smart camper on the trading field.

Here's a checklist of what questions should be answered in the introductory or overview section of your written trading plan:

1. What is my electronic trading philosophy or style? Am I a long-, medium-, or short-term trader? Clearly state your style—E-DAT scalper, day trader, swing trader, technician, etc. Then describe it, so there is no doubt in your mind.
2. What are my goals? Have I broken them down into per hour, per day, per week or per trade goals? Are they realistic?
3. Am I psychologically and financially suited for electronic trading?
4. How do I plan on keeping a trading diary? Database of trades?
5. How do I plan to select trades? Close out or offset trades? What is my analysis technique?
6. What strategies suit my resources?

7. How many and which markets will I trade?

8. Are the answers to all of the above questions consistent?

As you write your plan, keep in mind that it is a living document. It changes as your experience increases, as markets change, and as you modify your trading style.

You should also begin at this stage to prepare a list of your limitations and needs. This can be anything from something personal, like discipline, to something physical, like quotation equipment, to something intellectual, like fundamental or technical research. Later in this chapter I discuss how you can use this list of shortcomings in your selection of a broker and brokerage firm.

Once you've written general, almost philosophical, answers to the eight questions listed above, you should prepare a list of specific trading rules to live and trade by. The purpose of these rules is to instill discipline into your trading. Your trading decisions are business decisions—treat them with the same cold logic you would use to address the refinancing of your home or managing your business.

TRADING RULES

Money management is the first subject to explore. Throughout this book, I have made reference to 1000-share lot trades. To those new to E-DAT, this may sound like a large trade. You need to begin to think about it in terms of the dollar amount at risk. If you train yourself to cut your losses quickly, you close losing trades when they are down $\frac{1}{16}$, $\frac{1}{8}$, or $\frac{1}{4}$. This equates to losses of $62.50, $125, and $250, respectively, on this size trade. On the other hand, your objective may be to make $250 or $500 per trade in a matter of minutes or even less.

Those traders with longer time horizons who expect to hold positions for a day or more should think in terms of small-size orders and large point moves. My point is you can only risk what you can afford to lose and still have enough risk capital to continue to trade. Think of trading as fly-fishing. You must cast continually. If you do not get a hit, you immediately reel in and cast again.

The most common mistake new traders make is holding losers. Time and again I have watched novices take a one, two, or even a three dollar loss waiting for a trade to turn around. That is a loss of several thousand dollars that should have been limited to a loss of less than one hundred dollars. The concept in E-DAT is to get out if you are wrong and let your profits run when you are right.

Think in terms of the risk-to-reward ratio. On the shortest-term trades, lasting two minutes or less, it is acceptable to use a one-to-one ratio. You risk ⅛ or ¼ to make ⅛ or ¼. It is even better to risk ⅛ to make ¼ for a two-to-one ratio. Never do it the other way around, i.e., risking ¼ to make ⅛. This may sound elementary, but I see traders doing it every day.

Use the concept of visualization as you calculate the risk-to-reward ratio. Let's say that today you plan on trading an earnings move. Dell is announcing earnings after the market closes, but rumor has it earnings are going to be better than expected. You visualize in your mind exactly what you think the stock will do. With that image in your mind, you go long. But the stock hesitates and takes a step back. What do you do? Panic? No, you instantly offset your position with a loss of a teenie (¹⁄₁₆). Dell did not perform as you had visualized it. You did not take the time to find out why. Once you close your position, you might want to spend a little time trying to learn what went wrong. Perhaps you just got in too early or Dell gave a warning that the Street's expectations were too high or an influential analyst changed his or her number—a lot can go wrong. Do not take the time to find out why until after you have protected yourself.

You can use visualization to avoid letting winners become losers. Using the Dell example again, you visualize Dell gaining three points because of its good earning news. Once you get in and the stock begins to climb, take your profit when it is offered. Instead of waiting for three, you might settle for two and one-half. Whatever you do, do not hold out for four, five, or six. Why? That's right, the smart money will be taking profit. And when they do, it will turn very fast, and the retracement can wipe out your profit as well.

There is a biblical parable about seven bad years following seven good years. I have often seen traders "trade in the zone," when everything they touch turns to gold. These hot streaks are often followed by equally cold periods. You need to learn how to deal with both. When you are in the zone, make the most of it. When your world turns to ice, pace yourself. Start by cutting down on the per share size of your trades. Or take a vacation from trading. Play a little golf or spend a day with your family. But whatever you do, do not press yourself. You will only burn out. Losing is part of trading. If you are in a losing streak, stop . . . regroup . . . go back to the basics . . . and begin to trade again slowly and very controlled. The magic will return. Trust me, I have been there.

When trading is going well, consider taking your original investment out of the market. Now you are trading only profits. This seems to take much of the pressure off some traders, and they trade in a more relaxed manner. I have seen it work.

Another big mistake I have seen traders do is to trade a strategy because there is some other motivation other than making a profit on the trade. There may be some tax angle they are playing or some other unrelated objective. Trade only to make a profit on each and every trade.

Time management is another key area to master. Never overtax yourself. If you honestly do not have time to prepare for the upcoming trading session or if there are more pressing issues on your mind, skip trading until you can commit your full mental and physical resources. If you do not have the time to do your homework, do not get into the market. Catch up first and then get back in. The flip side of this is paralysis through analysis, and you cannot execute a trade. Either extreme is equally destructive to successful trading.

One of the most difficult things for new traders to do is to trust their instincts and avoid listening to friends, fellow traders, and their broker. You must make your own decisions if you are ever going to make a go at electronic trading. It is wise to follow the rules you have learned in this book and to experiment with the strategies taught. As you do this you must develop your own way of trading and follow your own path. I have seen a lot of people make money in this business, but none have done it looking over someone else's shoulder. You will draw from many, but how you brew your own recipe for success is very personal.

E-DAT did not exist a few years ago. What does that tell you? You must be open to new ideas, more so in this area of trading than in just about any other. Technology is creating so many new trading opportunities that if you do not welcome change, you will be overwhelmed very quickly. Always try to be among the first to test and experiment with new ideas, equipment, and software. It is the only way to stay on top of this game.

One of the oldest axioms in the business, "The trend is your friend," means more when you are trading electronically than it does in just about any other way. The reason is that professionals trade before they have all the facts. This puts a premium on good instincts. Those that can feel what the market is doing have an advantage. Feeling what the market is doing is akin to trading with the trend. If a market leader jumps up two points, trade its close neighbors. For example, Microsoft leaps two points higher, go long Cisco or Intel. More likely than not, they will stay in lock step with Microsoft. When they do, take your profit fast. These are not planned trades. In most cases they are not even expected. They are gifts. Take them and run to the bank.

I have not said as much as I probably should have about trading with protective stops. This is as critical in electronic trading as it is in any other type of trading. The difference is, in most cases, the stops must be mental. The markets move too fast to place actual stops and the stops would be so near the bid or ask, they would always get hit. Nevertheless, the stops must be in your mind and your mind must be on the stock you are trading. Time and again, I ask traders why they took a loss of a point or more and their answer is simply that they allowed themselves to get distracted. That, in my opinion, is not an acceptable answer. If you have a problem with your attention span, forget electronic trading. It is not for you. Also, if you lose a point or a "stick," think of how many learning experiences you lost. If you cut your losses to "teenies," that is, 16 more round turns, you could have made and learned a lot. How much do you learn with one big loser? Not much!

Another skill a lot of traders have a hard time developing is trading short. We are all bulls at heart, as I mentioned earlier in this book. But as a member of our team and fellow trader, Kevin Ward, often reminds me, "It is easier to fall out of a tree, than it is to climb it." Markets fall faster than they ascend. The reason is few traders are comfortable with the short side of the market. We all can make up good reasons why a stock is going up, but when it is heading south, we are all at a loss. We never seem to know why until it is too late. Again, trade the trend. If the market leader takes a hit, look for the rest of that group to take a plunge—and shadow the move lower. If you wait for the rationale, you will miss the opportunity.

FINDING AN E-DAT FIRM

Now, let's talk a little about finding a good broker and a good brokerage firm. E-DAT is a hot medium. It is fast, not bound by any physical restrictions, and somewhat impersonal. To balance this very high-tech environment you will be trading in, look for a brokerage firm that is "high touch." High touch works best with high tech. A high touch firm goes out of its way to stay in contact with you. For example, they usually provide E-DAT training, on-going seminars, chat rooms on their Web site, and social meetings where you can meet other E-DAT traders and exchange ideas. Once you complete training, they may offer some type of communal trade facility where you can trade for a while with a mentor until you are ready to go at it on your own at home and on-line.

The broker may also have a permanent place to trade. Some traders do much better if they have a place to trade other than their home. It is like athletes putting on their game face once they enter the arena in which they are going to complete. I have also noticed a lot of synergism between traders. E-DAT traders are like the computer hackers of the 1980s and '90s, who freely shared information. It is not uncommon to see one trader develop an effective trading strategy and share it with everyone in the room. If you can find a high-touch brokerage firm that goes out of its way to develop a community of traders, rather than just signing up as many clients as it can, you are well on your way to a successful E-DAT career.

You should also be able to rely on your broker-dealer to keep you up-to-date on all the advances in electronic trading. New innovations are appearing daily. It is their responsibility to stay on top of the technology and share it with you. Additionally, you should expect them to provide you with access to them in whatever mode you prefer, i.e., telephone, e-mail, fax, etc. You also want access to a strong Web site that contains helpful trading information. It could be something as simple as a schedule of earnings reports or as complex as software you can download to your computer.

Now let's talk about selecting the firm. In most cases, E-DAT traders are independent. They do not rely on a broker as traditional traders do. Nevertheless, you may have need for one, particularly if you cannot trade full-time or you just want to use a brokerage firm that specializes in E-DAT trading. So let's talk about brokers in general.

A good broker is a broker who will satisfy your needs. That person must have more experience in direct access electronic trading than you do. You want him or her to teach you, not the other way around. By now, you know this type of trading is substantially different from traditional trading. The strategies are different, the speed is faster, the rules and discipline of traditional trading do not apply. A broker who is not totally committed to an electronic environment cannot coach you successfully.

Look for a broker who can provide you with whatever you are lacking. For example, if you need some technical analysis help, be sure that is one of the strengths of any broker you hire. Interview your broker-dealer as if you were hiring an employee. Ask all the pertinent questions, some of which we covered in Chapter 11.

As you interview brokers, test them. If they are not responsive when soliciting your business, you can be sure they won't be any better when they have it. Ask perspective brokers to e-mail you a list of all the corporations that will post earnings reports next month. When you get it, quiz the broker to find out if he or she knows what the whisper number is for a few of the stocks that are about to report. Try to get a feel for his or her understanding of how to trade these numbers. Just ask, "How would you trade in this situation?"

What you are after is an insight into how the broker can help you trade better and more efficiently. Ask if the broker trades his own account. Personally, I have mixed feelings about brokers trading for themselves. I worry that they will be more concerned about their own money than mine. On the other hand, a broker that has not traded is lacking in experience. It is like teaching pilots to dogfight without ever having been in one yourself. There is something missing. But if you are a very experienced trader, this is not as serious a disqualification as it is for the novice trader.

You also want to get as close a match as possible between your personality—and your broker's. If you are not in synchronization, you will be in total conflict at some point. It goes without saying that a broker should be honest, intelligent, responsive, reliable, and helpful. He or she should have an understanding of the paperwork and the ability to solve problems.

CONCLUDING COMMENTS

In conclusion, I would just like to answer the questions I am most commonly asked when I conduct seminars and training sessions. Here is a representative sample.

- **How reliable is electronic trading?**

I need to answer that on several levels. First is the computer you would be working on at home or your office. I cannot answer that for you, but I can tell you that it has not been a problem for any of our clients. You need a reliable Internet provider, telephone company, and computer. Additionally, it helps to have a second telephone line to call your broker or one of your service providers for help while the system is up. I also recommend a backup power supply for your computer. Also, be sure your broker, or someone at his or her firm, can step in and take you flat, if you do experience any serious problems. My answer would be that reliability has not been a problem with the Tradewise™ system powered by Cybertrader®.

- **You talked a lot about the speed of execution. Is this really an important issue?**

I personally think it is, especially if you are trading for small incremental profits. But the importance is really knowing you have been filled and that you can exit the trade just as quickly. This gives you tremendous confidence in your ability to be successful. It is a power rush that is hard to explain to anyone that has not had an order filled in a second or two.

- **Is it unrealistic for just anyone off the street to become an electronic trader overnight?**

Yes, it certainly is. First, you must have a certain passion for the market. You must want to be around it all day long. Then you need a certain knack for understanding the markets. Like any skill, you must learn the basics at a good trading school and fine-tune them on a trading simulator. Not everyone is suited for electronic trading full time, any more than everyone can write a song, fly a plane, or run a marathon. On the other hand, there are journeymen and master traders. Just about anyone who loves to trade can become, in my opinion, a journeyman electronic trader and make a great living at it. A few lucky traders will become masters and make fortunes.

- **How complicated is the trading software?**

I would classify all of the software programs mentioned in this book as being extremely user friendly. Remember, a broker must learn to use them. Seriously, they are basically intuitive. All you do is point, click, and drag—no complicated formulas to memorize. Nevertheless, you need time on a simulator because when you have to point, click, or drag, you may feel as if the weight of the world is on your shoulders, so learning to operate the software under pressure is important.

- **Do you have to be at your computer terminal all day long?**

That depends on your trading style. If you trade very short-term, you only need to be there while you have an open position. It is common to see E-DAT's trade for a couple of hours in the morning and leave in the afternoon. If you hold positions for a day or longer, a lot depends on your strategy, when you expect to exit the trade, and what your exit signal is. Your broker may be able to monitor your position. It all depends on your style and objectives.

Also keep in mind that when you are live with the markets, so is your phone line to your Internet access service. Once again I recommend you take special care in selecting an Internet service provider (ISP). Find one with either local access or a toll-free line. Also check to see what the ratio of users to phone lines is. This ratio should be 9:1, or one line for every nine users or lower. The ISPs are required to give you this ratio on request and many print it in their sales literature.

- **What markets are the best ones to start trading electronically?**

That is a function of the type of trading you plan on doing. For short-term momentum traders, think NASDAQ. It also lends itself to technical analysis. This market is set for the trader who trades heavy—large positions (1000+ shares), held for a very short period of time (as short as one or two minutes), looking for small incremental profits (⅛, ¼, or ½ of a point). The daily and weekly trade volume is high, often 10, 20, 50, and even over 100 trades per day. I personally consider the risk to be controlled because of the amount of time trades are held.

- **Are the systems secured? Is it safe to trade?**

At your end of the line, you need to make sure no one can access your account. After you make trades, your trade tickets print-out in your broker's office. If your computer and your trading programs are not password protected now, you should start using passwords. And, change them regularly.

Once your order is filled, it is sent to a clearinghouse. All of these clearinghouses have strong security, particularly fire walls and encryption software. Therefore, I feel good about most vendors available today.

- **Are there any special educational steps I should take or reading material?**

As mentioned earlier in the text, a good electronic trading school is a must for anyone new to this type of trading. That school must provide time on a simulator. As far as reading material, I still think the best book on speculation was written in 1923, *Reminiscences of a Stock Operator.*

- **How much capital is needed?**

Each brokerage firm has its minimum account requirement. That can range from $5,000 to over $100,000. Ours is $5,000. I think that is sufficient to get started on a conservative program, more money for active trading.

- **What other useful tips can I share?**

When shorting a stock, always check with your broker first to make sure stock is available to borrow, if you plan to hold the position overnight. I have seen times when stock was not available and the trader had to close the position before the closing bell. Remember, good software will have the short list built in.

Beginning traders should only make one trade at a time. From watching traders new to electronic trading, I have observed, that if they try to make multiple trades simultaneously, they have a much higher chance of losing on one or more trades. I think the reasons are simply not being able to keep track of all the information and having problems switching between stocks. This is a great skill to practice on a simulator.

One last thought I'd like to leave with you. You are able to compete with the top professionals you will be trading against. As a matter of fact, I think the scale is tilted in your favor for two reasons. First, the regulation pendulum has swung in your favor. You can SOES a market maker at will, and you can place limit orders in front of market makers—these are just two of the advantages you have, and for the first time in over 200 years, you have the keys to unlock the gates of Wall Street.

But the second reason is even more important in my view of the world of trading. You are trading your own money, not some giant corporation's. The Harris and Schultz study on SOES trading attributes the success of the SOES bandits to this very factor. When large corporations were first moving into agriculture, the question of their efficiency, compared to the family farm, was always questioned by asking, "Who will stay up all night with the corporate sow when she is farrowing?" Now I ask, "Who pays more attention to their trading than individual traders with their own hard-earned money at risk?"

Before concluding with the Afterword of this book, I would like to comment on the subject of connectivity.

CONNECTIVITY

The telecommunications business has been the backbone of the entire technical revolution. Without it there would not be an Internet, 56K modems, or on-line trading, which didn't even begin until mid-1996. The boom has come a long way in an unbelievably short period of time, all because of the Internet.

Research, earnings consensus estimates, split announcements, ratings changes, and direct access have come to the average person who wants to trade like a pro. I have been in many of my friends' and clients' homes that have trading rooms that attempt to mimic a mini-Wall Street! All this because of connectivity and the Internet.

The question that should be on your mind is where to begin. I would tell you that firms such as my firm, Market Wise Trading, Inc., and schools are available to give you many options to get a direct connection to this technology. The question is: How serious do you want to get?

Let's start with a few broad options you have to get true access to the market with an E-DAT system:

In-house trading room at a broker-dealer

Internet connection to a broker-dealer

Remote access server (RAS) connection to a broker-dealer, and

Satellite connection to your broker-dealer

IN-HOUSE FLOOR TRADING

I will start with the first option and cover the pros and cons of each. Trading in-house on a trading floor at an existing office is very exciting and a huge learning experience for most new traders. You are able to interact with the instructors that have taught you to trade as well as to be around other traders who are there to synergize with.

Some of the disadvantages would be that this technology is so cutting-edge that many geographical barriers may exist. If there is no branch office of a broker-dealer near you, the access to this environment would not exist. Because there are so few true E-DAT trading offices across the country, this can be an obstacle. In addition, the cost to sit at one of these firms can be very expensive, and there is often minimum trade volume required which can be a problem for the new, fledgling trader.

If you are fortunate enough to live near such a firm that also meets your criteria and expectations in terms of support and pro-

fessionalism, this is an outstanding place to begin. Seating availability will tend to be a problem, but many offer special arrange-
ments for active traders.

INTERNET ACCESS

Connecting via the Internet offers many choices which can be as simple as you want to make it or as confusing as you would ever want
to imagine. There are tier 1, 2, and 3 Internet providers. A tier 1
provider is the best with the cleanest connection. There are DSL connections, ISDN line connections, cable modems, line ratios, and a
host of other considerations. One common denominator is that the
Internet will be here to stay for E-DAT. Some firms shoot down the
theory of trading on the Net, but the growth of this industry is undeniable. I suspect firms that shy away from this medium lack the technology to support their product on the Internet.

The Internet does have its problems, however. ISPs often
oversubscribe their capacity to support customers due to the ratio
of phone lines per customer. I would stay away from any provider
with a greater than 9 customer per line ratio. There are bottleneck
issues when trading traffic is high, occasional slow quotes, which is
vital for a real-time E-DAT. Being bumped off-line in the middle of
a trade is certainly an issue as well. Using the best ISP is highly
important.

The ways of creating redundancy through a separate phone
line and choosing a broker-dealer that takes your calls quickly when
problems as mentioned above occur are two solutions that can ward
off 95% of any potential problem you would have. But even with
this redundancy it still requires careful planning in connectivity.
Should you pay up for an ISDN line, upgrade your modem, invest
in a cable modem, go the DSL route, shop ISPs, etc.? My suggestion
is to speak very closely with the E-DAT broker-dealer you choose
and ask for assistance in these matters. A quality firm will support
you in getting these answers for you in order to earn your valuable
business. Finally, find out which "backbone" provider your firm
uses, and use the same ISP.

REMOTE ACCESS SERVERS (RAS)

A Remote Access Server (RAS) is a solution for people who are within a local telephone call to a broker-dealer who offers this option. This creates the best of both worlds in terms of a dedicated circuit that alleviates the problems the Internet can have, while still giving you the ability to trade from home or the office. This is also an option that is available for the trader who does not mind paying for a long-distance phone call to dial directly into the broker-dealer's network. The connection with an RAS is very clean, but costs a little more per month. I would choose this option if I could dial in locally myself.

The RAS is a dedicated phone line that will be set up on both ends, where your broker-dealer will provide a line for you to dial in on with your computer. The connection will link you directly to the network that the firm uses for its house traders, but with the benefit of a remote connection. The feeds tend to be a bit faster and the downtime by comparison to the Internet is reduced.

SATELLITE CONNECTIONS

The Internet continues to evolve, and now there are satellite connections to allow the E-DAT to connect over the Internet but through a satellite. This connection tends to be a faster connection than traditional land lines and will help diminish the problems associated with ISP. The cost is more because of hardware that needs to be purchased, but when you are trading your money, it is probably worth the investment.

Connectivity issues should be some of the questions you ask when inquiring about an account at a firm. Among my list of questions would be:

- Training classes
- Account information, such as money market, compliance, and margin
- Software and fail-safes for avoiding costly errors
- Connectivity options

- Broker and technical support when the system goes down
- Account statements and the ease of reading them. This is very important, given some of the poor statements that are out there.
- Continuing education, Web site support, and research

All these considerations are important when choosing a firm. Do the research on the front end, so that you have no worries later. Your head needs to be in trading, and not in constantly overcoming obstacles that could have been prevented by due diligence.

AFTERWORD

THE FUTURE OF E-DAT

S creen-based markets are the fastest-growing segment of the stock market, and the future has never looked brighter for the individual electronic trader. In fact, I cannot think of a better time to be alive than right now!

It is the turn of, not just a century, but a millenium! That is hard to comprehend when you really think about it. So take a deep breath, sit back in your chair and ask yourself this question, "Where do I want to go with E-DAT?"

If you answer, "To the next level!" than hold on—the trip promises to be as dynamic as the market itself.

The NASDAQ was proactive in sharing their proposed changes submitted to the SEC for a new order-delivery system that will create a more efficient and fairer market for all participants. With the recent rule changes covered in this book, we have already seen extensive changes swinging the pendulum in the direction of a fairer market for all participants, such as the Limit Order Protection Rule. Now additional changes are on the horizon. Let's take a walk into the future and take a look at some of these proposals.

New proposed rules will replace the current SOES and Select-Net functions with a system that will keep some elements of both and eliminate some functions that have been deemed unfair to market participants, including you, not just the industry professionals.

The most striking change, if approved by the SEC, will be the creation of a voluntary Limit Order File, enabling participants to obtain rapid executions through market makers and ECNs in a new NASDAQ Limit Order File (LOF), which would be similar to the Level II screen. Essentially, this puts the market makers and ECNs on level footing; both would be required to honor their quotes, if the quote is the inside market. This is a major change in that if you, as a trader, bid a stock with an ECN and make the high bid, any order to sell at your quoted price will be automatically filled. This is important because you would bid for stock only when you actually want it. Therefore, this substantially increases your liquidity—beyond the ECN—into the entire LOF, which is an integrated system of all the order books. Liquidity for the individual trader should skyrocket!

Another proposed change is the size of order that can be entered on the LOF. It will accept orders from 1 to 999,999 shares. Additional requirements for the market makers and ECNs with these new tier sizes will surely develop as the review continues. Orders on the proposed system will also be designated *direct* and *indirect*. Directed orders will work like a SelectNet preference order currently does, where a trader or market maker can direct a bid or offer (negotiation) to a specific firm, ECN, or market maker. Directed orders will not appear on the LOF or on NASDAQ's montage (Level II screen), just as SelectNet negotiations do not appear on Level II today.

Indirect orders will be sent to the LOF, just as they are now sent to ECNs who are able to take high bids and low offers on the Level II screen. Essentially, one primary function of these new proposed rules is to integrate SOES, SelectNet, and ECNs into a single system. I think this is great since it increases liquidity for us, the traders, and that is the most important element of a vibrant market.

Since SOES was developed in 1984 and SelectNet in January of 1988, many changes have taken place on NASDAQ. These new rules will not significantly change the way trading is done electronically, but they will help to create a more vibrant market, offering market participants added liquidity and ease of execution. I believe that this new integrated system, which is to be implemented in mid-1999, and the merger of the screen-based NASDAQ with the floor-based AMEX, will create even more opportunity for E-DAT traders. The proposed rule changes may seem a bit complex. If you wish to read more about these changes, you can do so by visiting the NASDAQ Web site: **www.nasdaqtrader.com**.

SOES and SelectNet may change form and be replaced. ECNs will be improved and take on more responsibility, but screen-based markets are here to stay. And you can hear NASDAQ grow as you read this book. It has announced a merger with the AMEX and by this book's press time, I would not be surprised if the Philadelphia or other regional exchanges have joined as well.

Systems like OptiMark will challenge the NYSE and provide new liquidity in the market for listed securities. Such systems will eventually become the ultimate screen-based trading vehicle.

Conditional trade entry systems are already in development stages. They will allow you to put conditions, such as price, size, etc., on orders. New software programs will execute trades for you while you are at work, playing golf, or spending valuable time with your family. The order-execution strategies allow for more absentee management trading. Traders who crave the need to point and click their way interactively to profits will have access to improved technology. These systems will allow for more "price improvement" through anonymous trading procedures. Program trading, such as that used by institutions daily to automatically take advantage of arbitrage opportunities, will become available to individuals.

Cellular modems are already common. You can trade from the beaches of Hawaii or the Olympics in Salt Lake City! Yes, technology is here to stay and the paradigms of Wall Street have broken down and embraced the evolution of the future. But let's not forget another side of the equation, the human element—the most fascinating and complex element of all!

Technology will continue to play a vital role. But as long as human beings are involved in the market—which I believe will be as long as we are capitalists—the driving force will be psychology, discipline, attitude, knowledge, and taking responsibility for our actions. These are the human qualities that define the successful trader. As long as you continue to develop your personal skills, in unison with technology, you will be in a position to reap huge rewards in the markets.

I am the kind of trader who sees the market as a "market of opportunity," not because I am any smarter but because that is the attitude I choose to embrace. The future of E-DAT is still inside you and how you choose to develop within the industry. If you want unlimited success, it is there. If you expect failure, it is there as well. It isn't a coincidence that trading today is very much like it was in the roaring 1920s. History does and will repeat itself, and the more things change the more they stay the same! Earl Nightingale said it best, "The fact is and always has been, that we really do become what we think about."

The mind isn't that different than our stomachs in the sense that we become what we feed ourselves. My brother once said, and I will always remember it, some people like "junk food for the mind and others choose to be gourmets." What will you feed your mind? My suspicion is that you will feed it with knowledge that will replace fear with confidence. That you will feed your attitude to generate results and will continue to improve your discipline to ultimately take control of your financial decisions and future. I feel that way because you already have taken the time to read this book, for which I congratulate you! This already puts you ahead of 90 percent of the general public.

So let me conclude by saying that you must continue to develop as the technology continues to grow at an unprecedented pace. The technology you need to trade directly with the market will change, but the attitude you take and the confidence you need will always be the same.

I am going to close on a philosophical note. I hope you find happiness in trading the way I have, and so many of my friends have, but remember true wealth is found in other areas. For me, the four precepts to true happiness are:

- Marry the right spouse
- Live where you love waking up
- Take care of your children
- Make your living doing what you love

May you find not just your financial bank account overflowing but also your emotional one. Good luck and TradeWise in the 21st century!

APPENDIX A

THE MARKET MAKERS AND THEIR SYMBOLS

Aegis Capital Corp.	AGIS	Hambrecht & Quist Inc.	HMQT
Alex Brown & Sons	ABSB	Herzog, Heine, Geduld	HRZG
Bear Stearns & Co.	BEST	J.P. Morgan Securities Inc.	JPMS
Bernard Madoff	MADF	Jeffries Co. Inc.	JEFF
BT Securities Corp.	BTSC	Kemper Securities Inc.	KEMP
Cantor Fitzgerald & Co.	CANT	Lehman Brothers	LEHM
Carlin Equities Corp.	CLYN	M.H. Meyerson & Co.	MHMY
CJLawrence/Deutsche	CJDB	Mayer Schweitzer Inc.	MASH
Coastal Securities LTD.	COST	Merrill Lynch & Co.	MLCO
Cowen & Co.	COWN	Midwest Stock Exchange	MWSE
CS First Boston	FBCO	Montgomery Securities	MONT
Dain Bosworth Inc.	DAIN	Morgan Stanley	MSCO
Domestic Securities Inc.	DOMS	Nash Weiss	NAWE
Donaldson, Lufkin, Jenrette	DLJP	Needham & Co.	NEED
ExponentialCapitalMarkets	EXPO	NomuraSecuritiesInt'l., Inc.	NMRA
Fahnestock & Co.	FAHN	Olde Discount Corp.	OLDE
First Albany Corp.	FACT	Oppenheimer & Co.	OPCO
Fox-Pitt, Kelton Inc.	FPKI	Paine Webber	PWJC
Furman Selz Inc.	SELZ	Pershing Trading Company	PERT
Goldman Sachs & Co.	GSCO	Piper Jaffray Inc.	PIPR
Gruntal & Co.	GRUN	Prudential Securities Inc.	PRUS
GVR Co.	GVRC	Punk Ziegel & Knoell Inc.	PUNK

Ragen McKenzie Inc.	RAGN	Troster Singer	TSCO
RauscherPierce Refsnes Inc.	RPSC	Tucker Anthony Inc.	TUCK
Robertson Stephens & Co.	RSSF	UBS Securities Inc.	UBSS
S.G. Warburg & Co. Inc.	WARB	Volpe Welty	VOLP
Salomon Brothers	SALB	Wallstreet Equities Inc.	WSEI
Sands Brothers Inc.	SBNY	WedbushMorgan Securities	WEDB
Sherwood Securities Corp.	SHWD	Weeden & Co. LP	WEED
Smith Barney Shearson	SBSH	Wertheim Shroder & Co.	WERT
SoundviewFinancial Group	SNDV	WeselsArnold & Henderson	WSLS
Southwest Securities Inc.	SWST	Wheat First Securities Inc.	WEAT
Teevan & Co.	TVAN	William Blair & Co.	WBLR

KNOW YOUR MARKET MAKER

Here are a few firms to watch closely while trading. If you want to learn more about these firms, study their Internet Web sites.

INSTITUTIONAL FIRMS

These firms generally have a global presence and participate in the largest underwritings. They mainly cater to the major institutions, such as mutual funds and pension plans. They generate the best market research, primarily fundamental analysis. The market makers are 900-pound gorillas, so don't trade against any of these heavyweights!

GSCO	GOLDMAN SACHS & CO.
SALB	SALOMON BROTHERS
LEHM	LEHMAN BROTHERS
MSCO	MORGAN STANLEY

WHOLESALERS

These firms do not research stocks or have any bias in a given stock. They simply make a market for other firms. They conduct no retail business.

MASH	MAYER AND SCHWEITZER
HRZG	HERTZOG HEIN & GEDULD

TSCO	TROSTER SINGER
SHWD	SHERWOOD
NITE	KNIGHT
MHMY	MH MAYERSON

WIRE HOUSES

These are the large retail, full-service brokerage firms. They have financial advisers and registered reps (brokers) whose primary job is to generate commissions and order flow.

SBSH	SMITH BARNEY SHEARSON
DEAN	DEAN WITTER REYNOLDS
PAIN	PAINE WEBBER
PRUD	PRUDENTIAL
MLCO	MERRILL LYNCH & CO

REGIONAL FIRMS

These are the smaller brokerage firms, with relatively less exposure in the market. They watch every trade, like the individual traders do. They are more market sensitive than the larger firms.

PIPR	PIPER JAFFREY
SWST	SOUTH WEST
DAIN	DAIN, BOSWORTH INC.
WEAT	WHEAT, FIRST SECURITIES

INVESTMENT BANKS

These firms are strictly in the business of underwriting. They help companies complete IPOs and secondary offerings. They are not primary market makers; however, they generally trade stocks that they underwrite.

HMQT	HAMBRECHT and QUIST
MONT	MONTGOMERY
COWN	COWEN

E-DAT TRADER'S QUICK REFERENCE GUIDE TO UNDERSTANDING THE LEVEL II SCREEN

Buy Side

High Bid
A market maker enters a bid at a price higher than the current inside or best-bid level.

Join the Bid
A market maker enters a bid at the current high-bid level.

Sell Throughs
Transactions are being executed above the low offer.

Leave the Offer
A market maker removes its offer to sell from the low offer price level.

Volume on Bid
A market maker or ECN shows a large volume of stock to buy at the high-bid level.

Ax on the Bid
A leading market maker that consistently shows up at the high bid.

Refresh the Bid
A market maker reinputs its bid at the high-bid level after being hit by a SOES execution.

Lift the Offer
A market maker lifts a SelectNet offer at the low offer price, i.e., pays retail for stock.

Sell Side

Low Offer or Ask
A market maker enters an offer at a price lower than the current inside or best-offer level.

Join the Offer
A market maker enters an offer at the current low offer level.

Buy Throughs
Transactions are being executed below the high bid.

Leave the Bid
A market maker removes its bid from the high-bid price level.

Volume on Ask
A market maker or ECN shows a large volume of stock for sale at the low-ask level.

Ax on the Ask or Offer
A leading market maker that consistently shows up at the low offer.

Refresh to Ask or Offer
A market maker reinputs its offer at the low offer level after being hit by a SOES execution.

Hit on the Bid
A market maker hits a SelectNet bid at the high-bid price level, i.e., sells stock at wholesale.

GLOSSARY OF ELECTRONIC TRADING AND WALL STREET TERMS

The following is a glossary of useful terms for the electronic trader, plus some Wall Street lingo you should be aware of.

ADR (American Depository Receipt):   A negotiable receipt for a given number of shares of a foreign corporation. Traded on U.S. exchanges just like shares of stock.

ADX: A mathematical formula that measures trend strength in either direction. ADX will use +DI or −DI (directional indicators) to determine directional bias. This information is available through Bloomberg.

Advance/decline line: Represents the total difference between advances and declines of security prices. Considered the best indicator of market movement as a whole.

AON (all or none order):   An order in which the floor broker is instructed to execute the entire order in one transaction.

Arbitrage: Simultaneous sales and purchases in the same or equivalent securities to take advantage of market inefficiency.

Arbitrageur: One who engages in arbitrage.

At the money: An option in which the underlying stock is trading exactly at the exercise price of the option.

Basis point: Equal to 1/100 of 1 percent of yield (e.g., ½% = 50 basis points)

Beta: A means of measuring the volatility of a stock in comparison to the market as a whole. A beta of 1 indicates that a stock will move with the market. A beta higher than 1 means the stock has higher volatility than the market as a whole.

Bid: An indication by an investor, a trader, or a dealer of a willingness to buy a security at a given price.

Block trade: A trade of 10,000 shares or more.

Blue chip: The issues of normally strong, well-established companies that have demonstrated their ability to pay dividends in good and bad times.

Bull market: A market in which prices are moving higher or are expected to move higher.

Call: An option contract giving the owner the right to buy stock at a stated price within a specified period of time.

CFO (cancel former order):   An instruction by a customer to cancel a previously entered order or change one or more of the terms.

Cash account: An account in which a client is required to pay in full for securities purchased.

Chicago Board Options Exchange (CBOE):   The first national securities exchange for the trading of listed options.

Common stock: An equity security that represents ownership in a corporation.

Consumer price index (CPI):   A measure of inflation or deflation based on price changes in consumer goods.

Cost to carry: All out-of-pocket costs incurred by the investor to hold a position.

CUSIP: The unique 9-character serial number of a registered security.

Defensive strategy: An investment method whereby an investor seeks to minimize the risk of losing principal. The policy of making purchases and sales according to predetermined objectives without regard for market changes.

Delta: A term used to describe the responsiveness of option premiums to a change in the price of the underlying asset. Deep in-the-money options have a delta near 1; these show the biggest response to price changes. Deep out-of-the-money options have very low deltas.

Discretionary account: An account in which the owner of the assets has given the broker or other representative the authority to make transactions at the representative's discretion.

DK (don't know): A term indicating a lack of knowledge about a transaction between broker-dealers.

DVP (delivery versus payment): A transaction settlement method in which the securities are delivered to the buying institution's bank in exchange for payment of the amount due.

EPS (earnings per share): The net income of a company divided by the number of shares of common stock outstanding.

Equity: The ownership interest of common and preferred stockholders in a corporation; also the client's net worth in a margin account.

Exercise: The implementation of the rights of an option or warrant.

Exercise price: The price per share at which the holder of an option (call or put) or warrant may buy or sell the underlying security.

Expiration date: The specified date on which an option becomes worthless and the holder no longer has the rights specified in the contract.

Federal Funds Rate: The interest rate charged by one institution lending overnight funds to another.

Federal Reserve Board: A seven-member group appointed by the president to oversee operation of the Federal Reserve System.

FOK (fill or kill order): An order that instructs the floor broker to fill the entire order immediately or cancel the entire order. Partial fills are not acceptable.

Fourth market: The trading of securities directly between institutional investors without the services of a broker, primarily through the use of InstiNet.

Open order: Unfilled order still in the market.

Gross national product (GNP): The total value of goods and services produced by a country during one year.

Growth stock: A relatively speculative issue, usually paying little or no dividends and selling at a high price/earnings ratio.

GTC (good till canceled order): An order that is left in force until it is executed or canceled.

Inside information: Material or nonpublic information obtained or used by a person for the purpose of trading in a security.

Inside market: For any given OTC stock at a given point in time, the inside market is the best bid (highest) price at which stock can be sold in the inter-dealer market and the best ask (lowest) price at which the same stock can be bought.

InstiNet: An electronic system owned by Reuters Holdings, PLC, that offers its subscribers a means of trading over 10,000 issues without using a broker-dealer or going through an exchange.

IOC (immediate or cancel order): An order instructing the floor broker to execute immediately. Any portion remaining unfilled is canceled. Partial fills are acceptable.

IPO (initial public offering): A company's initial public offering, referred to as "going public," is the first sale of stock by the company to the public.

In the money: An option that has intrinsic value.

Intrinsic value: The mathematical value of an option. A call is said to have intrinsic value when the stock is trading above the exercise price. A put has intrinsic value when the stock is trading below the exercise price.

Level I: The basic level of NASDAQ service, which provides real-time bid and ask quotations on NASDAQ stocks.

Level II: Provides real-time inside bid and ask quotations and the bid and ask quotations of each market maker for a given security.

Level III: The highest level of NASDAQ service. Offers the same quotation service of Level II, but allows each market maker to enter and change their quotes.

Liquidity: The ease with which something can be bought or sold in the marketplace. A large number of buyers and sellers, combined with high volume, are important components of liquidity.

Long: The state of owning a security.

Major Market Index: A 20-stock index designed to track the DJIA. The Major Market Index is composed of 15 of the DJIA stocks and 5 other large NYSE listed stocks.

Margin account: An account in which the broker-dealer loans some of the purchase price of securities to the client, increasing the client's buying power.

MIC (market impact cost): The cost incurred when a market maker, or some other buyer or seller, such as a pension or mutual fund, has a large order to fill and, in the process drives the market up or down while buying or selling the stock.

Minus tick: An execution price below the previous sale price. A short sale cannot be executed on a minus tick, which is the same as a downtick.

NASDAQ 100: An index of the largest 100 nonfinancial stocks on NASDAQ weighted by capitalization.

Odd lot: Less than 100 shares of stock.

Odd lot theory: A technical theory based on the assumption that the investing public is always wrong. If odd-lot buying is up, the public is buying stock. The theory would indicate that the market is headed for a decline.

Offer: An indication by an investor, a trader, or a dealer of a willingness to sell a security at a given price. It is the same as an ask.

Option: The right to buy or sell a specified number of shares at a specified price within a specified time.

Out of the money: A term referring to an option which has no intrinsic value.

Overbought: An analyst's opinion that more and stronger buying has occurred in a market than the market fundamentals would justify.

Oversold: An analyst's opinion that more and stronger selling has occurred in a market than the market fundamentals would justify.

PE ratio (Price to earnings ratio): The ratio of the current market value of a stock divided by the annual earnings per share (EPS).

Plus tick: An execution price above the previous sale price.

Position: The amount of a security either owned (long position) or owed (short position) by an individual.

Price/earnings theory: The theory that attempts to determine the value of a stock based on its price to earnings ratio.

Put: An option contract that gives the owner the right to sell a specified number of shares at a specified price within a specified period of time.

REIT (real estate investment trust): Investment trusts, which are in direct ownership of income properties or mortgage loans. REITs are traded like stocks.

Resistance: A term used to describe the top of a stock's trading range.

Right: A security representing a stockholder's right to purchase new shares in proportion to the number of shares already owned.

Scalper: A short-term trader who buys and sells throughout the day in order to profit from small price changes in a security. Scalpers contribute greatly to the liquidity of the market.

Short sale: The sale of a security that the seller does not own, in hopes of profiting from a downward move in the stock's price.

SOES (Small Order Execution System): NASD's automatic order-execution system designed to favor small public market and executable limit orders.

SOES automatically matches and executes orders, locks in a price and sends confirmation directly to the broker-dealers on both sides of the trade. Institutions and broker-dealers may not employ SOES to trade for their own accounts. Only public-market orders and executable limit orders are accepted by SOES.

S&P 500 (Standard & Poor's 500 Composite Stock Price Index): A market index composed of 400 industrial stocks, 20 transportation stocks, 40 financial stocks, and 40 utility stocks. The S&P 500 is one of the most widely followed of the market indices.

Stock ahead: A limit order that is not filled because other orders at that same price were entered before that order. In this instance, the client will receive a report back saying, "stock ahead."

Straddle: A position consisting of a call and a put on the same security with the same strike price and expiration date. Straddles can be either long or short.

Strike price: The price at which the underlying security will be sold if the holder exercises an option.

SuperDot (Super Designated Order Turnaround System): The NYSE's computerized trading and execution system. Using SuperDot, an order can be routed directly to the appropriate specialist at his trading post on the floor of the exchange. Once the order is executed, the specialist can then use the same automated routing system to send an execution report back to the firm that submitted the order. Orders executed through the SuperDot system are usually confirmed in less than 60 seconds.

Support: A term used to describe the bottom of a stock's trading range.

Tick: This is a very short-term trading indicator. It is the difference between the number of NYSE stocks trading at a price higher than the previous trade ("uptick") and the number of stocks trading at a lower price than the previous trade ("downtick"). That is, tick equals the number of stocks moving higher minus the number of stocks moving lower. The number usually ranges between −600 and +600. A large positive tick generally means the market is attracting more buyers than sellers. The opposite is true of a large negative number. The direction of the tick is important. If it is moving in a positive direction (−100, 0, +150), the market is moving upward. If the tick is moving in a negative direction (+100, 0, −150), the market is going down.

Third market: The trading of exchange-listed securities in the OTC market.

Time value: A term used to describe the value of an option over and above its intrinsic value.

Warrant: A security giving the holder the right to purchase shares at a stipulated price up until a specified date.

APPENDIX C

MARKET INDICATORS,
USEFUL WEB SITES,
EXCHANGES, AND BOOKS

MARKET INDICATORS

AME: The American Stock Exchange Market Value Index includes all common stocks listed on the American Stock Exchange.

ARMS Index: These used to be called the *Trin,* or the short-term trading index. It is the ratio of the quotient of advancing issues divided by declining issues and up volume divided by down volume.

$$\frac{\text{Advancing issues/up volume}}{\text{Declining issues/down volume}} = \text{ARMS Index}$$

The direction of the ARMS Index is most important. A falling ARMS signals a strong market, while a rising ARMS suggests weakness ahead. The normal range is from 0.5 to 2.0.

BKX: The Philadelphia Stock Exchange/Keefe, Bruyette & Woods Bank Sector index is composed of stocks designed to represent national money center banks and leading regional institutions. BancOne, Citicorp, and Wells Fargo are among the 24 stocks in this index.

Dow Jones Industrial Average (DJIA):   It is also referred to as "the Dow." The Average is calculated using a formula and the common stock prices of 30 major U.S. industrial companies listed on the New York Stock Exchange.

Dow Jones Transportation Average: It is calculated using the prices of 20 airline, trucking, and railroad company stocks.

Dow Jones Utility Average: It contains the 15 gas, electric, and power company stocks on the Dow.

Dow Jones 65 Composite Average (DJCOM):   It is calculated from the average of all the stocks in the Dow Jones industrial, transportation, and utility averages.

NIKKEI: This stock average (pronounced "Nick-Kay") is an index of 225 high-quality blue-chip stocks on the Tokyo Stock Exchange; the Nikkei is Japan's equivalent of the Dow Jones Industrial Average.

NMS COMP: NASDAQ's National Market System Composite is an index of all issues traded over the counter on the NASDAQ National Market System.

NY ADV: The number of NYSE stocks that have increased in price from the previous day's close.

NY DEC: The number of NYSE stocks that have decreased in price from the previous day's close.

NY DN: The number of shares that have been traded for NYSE stocks that have decreased in price from the previous day's close.

NYSE Composite Index: It is a capitalization-weighted index of all common stocks listed on the New York Stock Exchange used as the basis for options and futures traded on the New York Stock Exchange.

NY TOT: The total number of shares that have been traded in NYSE stocks during the current trading day.

NY UNCH: The number of NYSE stocks trading at the same price as the previous day's close.

NY VOL UP: The number of shares that have been traded for NYSE stocks that have increased in price from the previous day's close.

OEX: Known as the S&P 100. It is used by the Chicago Board Options Exchange to trade stock index options.

PREM Value Index: It is useful in determining when computer-driven "buy" or "sell" programs are likely. Through computer programs, traders take advantage of premiums or discounts between the current price of stocks and stock index futures. Comparing the actual index to the futures contract, a trader will quickly sell the more expensive of the two and buy the less expensive. This computer-based activity (known as "program trading") can often accentuate sudden swings in the price of certain stocks, or cause dramatic shifts in the entire market. In general, when a significant premium exists, buy programs are likely to occur. When a significant discount exists, sell programs are likely. As a contract moves toward expiration, the difference between the future and cash prices will diminish. As a result, the premium or discount needed for a buy or sell program will also get smaller.

SOX: The Philadelphia Stock Exchange's Semiconductor Sector index measures the performance of some of the largest and most widely held U.S. computer chip stocks. This price-weighted index is made up of 16 stocks, including Intel, Micron Technology, and Texas Instruments.

Standard & Poor's 500 Index (S&P 500):   It is calculated using the stock prices of 500 relatively large companies as measured by capitalization. The S&P 500 is widely used as an indicator of stock market trends and for futures trading strategies. The components of the index can change, as S&P adds or deletes stocks to reflect changing conditions. The S&P's 500 is also broken down into smaller industry segments, which are monitored separately. These segments are industrial (400 companies), transportation (20 companies), utilities (40 companies), and financial (40 companies).

30-YR YLD: It is the yield of the most recently issued 30-year U.S. Treasury bond. This is widely used as a benchmark for long-term interest rates.

WSX: The Wilshire Small Cap Index measures the performance of companies with relatively small capitalizations. It is a market-weighted index that includes 250 stocks, chosen on the basis of their market capitalization, liquidity, and industry group representation. The small cap index originates from the Wilshire Next 1750 Index, a benchmark for institutional investors in the small cap sector.

XAU: The Gold and Silver Index is comprised of seven stocks on the New York and American Stock Exchanges. Some investors consider gold to be a "safe haven." As a result, its price often goes up in times of inflation, international finance crises, and threats of war.

XOI: The AMEX Oil Index includes 16 oil stocks. An increase can indicate rising oil prices, which may lead to increased inflation.

USEFUL WEB SITES

The following is a list of Web sites popular among E-traders. I highly recommend that you frequent them often for continued growth and ideas.

Nyse.com	Zacks.com
Sec Edgar.com	Bloomberg.com
Stock Investor Trading News	Moneynet.com
NASDAQ.com	Phlx.com
NASDAQtrader.com	

Of course, there are many other resources for information, but this is an excellent start for filling your brain with "mind food." If you have trouble finding any of the sites, use the search function on your browser and enter the above name(s).

EXCHANGES

All exchanges have public information, public relations, marketing, or sales departments that prepare and distribute a wide variety of instructional material. Most of them conduct seminars to teach investors how to trade the options listed on their exchange. They are an excellent source of additional information.

American Stock Exchange
Derivative Securities
86 Trinity Place
New York, NY 10006
1-800-THE-AMEX
or 2, London Wall Buildings
    London Wall
    London EC2M 5SY ENGLAND
    44-71-628-5982

Chicago Board Options Exchange
LaSalle at Van Buren
Chicago, IL 60605
1-800-OPTIONS
(312) 786-5600

New York Stock Exchange
Options and Index Products
11 Wall Street
New York, NY 10005
1-800-692-6973
(212) 656-8533

The Options Clearing Corporation
440 South LaSalle Street
Suite 2400
Chicago, IL 60605
1-800-537-4258
(312) 322-6200

Pacific Stock Exchange
Options Marketing
115 Sansome Street, 7th Floor
San Francisco, CA 94104
1-800-TALK-PSE
(415) 393-4028

Philadelphia Stock Exchange
Philadelphia Board of Trade
(Foreign Currency Options)
1900 Market Street
Philadelphia, PA 19103
1-800-THE-PHLX
(215) 496-5404
or PHLX European Office
   39 King Street
   London EC2V 8DQ ENGLAND
   44-71-606-2348

Chicago Mercantile Exchange
Index & Option Market
International Monetary Market
30 South Wacker Drive
Chicago, IL 60606
(312) 930-8200

REGULATORY ORGANIZATIONS

National Association of Securities
  Dealers (NASD)
1735 K Street NW
Washington, D.C. 20006
(202) 728-8000

Securities and Exchange
  Commission (SEC)
450 Fifth Street NW
Washington, D.C. 20006
(202) 728-8233

BOOKS OF INTEREST TO E-DAT TRADERS

Reminiscences of a Stock Operator, by Edwin Lefevre, Reprinted in 1994
Stock Patterns for Day Traders, by Barry Rudd, 1998
The Electronic Day Trader, by Marc Friedfertig and George West, 1998
The Mind of a Trader: Lessons in Trading Strategy from the World's Leading Traders, by Alpesh B. Patel, 1998
Electronic Trading "TNT" I Gorilla Trading Stuff, by Joe Ross and Mark Cherlin, 1998

APPENDIX D

E-DAT TRADING SOFTWARE AND QUOTATION SERVICES

This is only a small sampling of the services available. All the major players maintain Web sites. Therefore a search of the Internet will be productive.

TRADING PLATFORMS

Advance GET was rated the best stock trading system by *Stocks & Commodities* magazine in 1994, 1995, 1996, and 1997. It uses a wide array of technical studies. To get a good idea of this program's capabilities download the demo from their Web site. It is available either with end-of-day prices for $2750 or on a real-time basis for a monthly lease of $210. Trading Techniques, 667 West Turkey Foot Lake Road, Akron, Ohio 44319 (330) 645-1230. Web site: **www.tradingtech.com**.

Real Tick III includes Townsend Analytics programs. Real Tick includes quote screens, charts, tables, news, option information, and a variety of technical analysis studies. Studies and quotes can be linked to Microsoft Excel to build bar charts. The program contains audio and visual alarms. See Web site: **www.taltrade.com**.

S&P Comstock has two levels of service available. Level I ($175/month) includes quotes, tickers, Turbo options, basic charting, and S&P global news. Level II ($225/month) includes all of Level I, plus Time and Sale screen, NASDAQ Level II screen, stock/options tech studies, and international access. See Web site: **www.comstockline.com**.

TradeWise, powered by Real Tick III, is one of the finest and most advanced trading programs. Through the Archipelago ECN it automatically seeks out the fastest and best route to fill your orders. You also really appreciate having access to the Island Order Book, which shows who, besides the market makers, are actively buying and selling. This is one of the best ways to keep track of the outside market. The Top Ten Gainers and Losers screens can be configured to include list, OTC, or a combination. Plus they can be set to show you price or volume gains and losses. This system even calculates your daily profit and loss status. And this is only a few of the features, like charts, technical analysis studies, a window to access your favorite Internet site, and much, much more. For more information or a free CD showing you the Level II screen in action, contact **www.getmarketwise.com**, or call 1-877-MKT-WISE. Market Wise Stock Trading School, LLC, 6343 West 120th Ave., Broomfield, CO 80020.

ATTAIN is a platform provided by ALL-TECH Investment Group, Inc. Harvey Houtkin, "The original SOES Bandit" as he is known, is the owner. They can be reached at: **www.attain.com**.

QUOTATION SOFTWARE SERVICES

DTN Real Time is a quotation service only. It provides complete quote packages for stocks, options, and futures. Their Web site is: **www.dtn.com**.

PC Quote offers five levels of real-time quotation services ranging from $75 to $300/month. You can research stocks, bonds, futures, options, and mutual funds. Advanced services include charts and advisory information. Refer to Web site: **www.pcquote.com**.

The following Web sites also have price quotes:

Briefing.Com	www.briefing.com
Data Broadcasting Online	www.dbc.com
Interquote	www.interquote.com

APPENDIX E

THE NASDAQ 100 INDEX: A TARGET OF OPPORTUNITY

This index constantly changes, so you must continuously check to find which stocks are on it. When a stock is added or dropped for the index, you can trade that occurrence as an upgrade or downgrade.

The NASDAQ 100 Index includes 100 of the largest U.S. nonfinancial companies listed on the NASDAQ National Market tier of the NASDAQ Stock Market. Launched in January 1985, each security on the index is proportionately represented by its market capitalization in relation to the total market value of the index. The index reflects NASDAQ's largest growth companies across major industry groups, including major players in high tech, airlines, automotive services, department stores, and healthcare.

All index components have a minimum market capitalization of $500 million and an average daily trading volume of at least 100,000 shares. Almost all companies in the index have over $1 billion in market value; $6 billion is the average. In addition, companies must have been listed on NASDAQ for a minimum of two years before they can be considered for inclusion.

The number of securities in the NASDAQ 100 Index makes it an effective vehicle for arbitrageurs and securities traders. At the Chicago Board Options Exchange the NASDAQ 100 Index is used as the basis for an index option known as NDX. Since 1993, it has become the third most actively traded securities index option in the United States, after the S&P 100 and the S&P 500. On the Chicago Mercantile Exchange investors can also purchase futures. As with options, both institutional and retail customers are participants.

Company Name	Symbol	Company Name	Symbol
3Com Corporation	COMS	Dell Computer Corporation	DELL
Adaptec, Inc.	ADPT	Dura Pharmaceuticals, Inc.	DURA
ADC Telecom. Inc.	ADCT		
Adobe Systems Inc.	ADBE	Electronic Arts Inc.	ERTS
ADTRAN, Inc.	ADTN	Electronics for Imaging, Inc.	EFII
Allied Waste Industries, Inc.	AWIN		
		Fastenal Company	FAST
Altera Corporation	ALTR	First Health Group Corporation	FHCC
American Power Conversion Corp.	APCC		
		Fiserv, Inc.	FISV
Amgen Inc.	AMGN	Food Lion, Inc.	FDLNB
Andrew Corporation	ANDW	FORE Systems, Inc.	FORE
Apple Computer, Inc.	AAPL	Gartner Group, Inc.	GART
Applied Materials, Inc.	AMAT	General Nutrition Companies, Inc.	GNCI
Apollo Group, Inc.	APOL		
Ascend Communications, Inc.	ASND	Genzyme Corporation	GENZ
		HBO & Company	HBOC
Atmel Corporation	ATML	Herman Miller, Inc.	MLHR
Autodesk, Inc.	ADSK	Immunex Corporation	IMNX
Bed Bath & Beyond Inc.	BBBY	Intel Corporation	INTC
Biogen, Inc.	BGEN	JACOR Communications, Inc.	JCOR
Biomet, Inc.	BMET		
BMC Software, Inc.	BMCS	Jefferson Smurfit Corporation	JJSC
Cambridge Technology Partners, Inc.	CATP		
		KLA-Tencor Corporation	KLAC
Centocor, Inc.	CNTO	Level III Communications, Inc.	LVLT
Chancellor Media Corporation	AMFM		
		Linear Technology Corporation	LLTC
Chiron Corporation	CHIR		
Cintas Corporation	CTAS	LM Ericsson Telephone Company	ERICY
Cisco Systems, Inc.	CSCO		
Citrix Systems, Inc.	CTXS	Maxim Integrated Products, Inc.	MXIM
Comcast Corporation	CMCSK		
Compuware Corporation	CPWR	McCormick & Company, Inc.	MCCRK
Concord EFS, Inc.	CEFT		
Corporate Express, Inc.	CEXP	MCI Communications Corporation	MCIC
Costco Companies Inc.	COST		
Cracker Barrel Country Store, Inc.	CBRL	Microchip Technology Incorporated	MCHP

Company Name	Symbol	Company Name	Symbol
Micron Electronics, Inc.	MUEI	Quantum Corporation	QNTM
Microsoft Corporation	MSFT	Quintiles Transnational Corp.	QTRN
Molex Incorporated	MOLX		
Netscape Communications Corp.	NSCP	Qwest Communications International, Inc.	QWST
Network Associates, Inc.	NETA	Reuters Group PLC	RTRSY
Nextel Communications, Inc.	NXTL	Rexall Sundown, Inc.	RXSD
		Ross Stores, Inc.	ROST
Nordstrom, Inc.	NOBE	Sigma-Aldrich Corporation	SIAL
Northwest Airlines Corporation	NWAC	Staples, Inc.	SPLS
		Starbucks Corporation	SBUX
Novell, Inc.	NOVL	Stewart Enterprises, Inc.	STEI
Oracle Corporation	ORCL	Sun Microsystems, Inc.	SUNW
Oxford Health Plans, Inc.	OXHP	Sybase, Inc.	SYBS
PACCAR Inc.	PCAR	Synopsys, Inc.	SNPS
PacifiCare Health Systems, Inc.	PHSYB	Tech Data Corporation	TECD
		Tele-Communications, Inc.	TCOMA
PanAmSat Corporation	SPOT	Tellabs, Inc.	TLAB
PairGain Technologies, Inc.	PAIR	US Office Products Company	OFIS
Parametric Technology Corporation	PMTC	Wisconsin Central Trans. Corp.	WCLX
Paychex, Inc.	PAYX	WorldCom, Inc.	WCOM
PeopleSoft, Inc.	PSFT	Worthington Industries, Inc.	WTHG
PhyCor, Inc.	PHYC		
QUALCOMM Incorporated	QCOM	Xilinx, Inc.	XLNX

INDEX

ABOUT THE AUTHOR

David S. Nassar is the President and CEO of Market Wise Trading, Inc., a broker-dealer and Member of the NASD. He is also the founder, and driving force, behind this securities firm's specialization in electronic direct access trading (E-DAT). This service is provided to investors and traders on-line, via the Internet and other forms of electronic data transmission, and through the firm's branch-office system.

David S. Nassar is also the founder and principal owner of Market Wise Stock Trading School, LLC. The school prepares students to trade on all the major stock markets, listed and NASDAQ, utilizing E-DAT. The Market Wise School has taught hundreds of people how to trade electronically, using state-of-the-art technologies and strategies. Students from across the country and from foreign countries have attended these courses.

Mr. Nassar is a frequent speaker on the markets and a regular guest on Denver's largest radio program featuring financial news, *Business for Breakfast*. The market insights shared by David have created many loyal listeners and clients.

Conducting seminars on electronic direct access trading keeps Mr. Nassar very busy. He is a Registered Financial Planner, Registered Representative, and Financial Principal, with over 12 years of securities experience. Mr. Nassar graduated from Kutztown University with a business degree in 1986, and is married with two boys.

For comments to the author, please e-mail: dnassar@getmarketwise.com.